DRAW

DRAWING
RELATIONSHIPS
AND WORK-GROUPS

C
🙰

PROJECTIVE PSYCHOLOGICAL
ASSESSMENTS PROPOSED AS A
WALDEN THESIS

This is the text of the original thesis titled: *Relationship between Myers-Brigg Type Indicator Types®️ and Projective Drawing Constructs*, which was submitted in partial fulfillment of the requirements for the degree of Master of Science Psychology by C. M. Peterson, November 2008.

DEDICATION

To John.

This is nothing but wilderness;

there is no dread.

Flee fro the prees and dwelle with sothfastnesse;
Suffyce unto thy thing, though it be smal,
For hord hath hate, and climbing tikelnesse,
Prees hath envye, and wele blent overal.
Savour no more than thee bihove shal,
Reule wel thyself that other folk canst rede,
And trouthe thee shal delivere, it is no drede.

Tempest thee noght al croked to redresse
In trust of hir that turneth as a bal;
Gret reste stant in litel besinesse.
Be war therfore to sporne ayeyns an al,
Stryve not, as doth the crokke with the wal.
Daunte thyself, that dauntest otheres dede,
And trouthe thee shal delivere, it is no drede.

The wrastling for this world axeth a fal.
Her is non hoom, her nis but wildernesse:
Forth, pilgrim, forth! Forth, beste, out of thy stal!

Know thy contree, look up, thank God of al;
Hold the heye wey and lat thy gost thee lede,
And trouthe thee shal delivere, it is no drede....

Explicit Le bon counseill de G. Chaucer.
(Truth, G. Chaucer.)

ACKNOWLEDGMENTS

I wish to express my deep appreciation for James Dean whose knowledge, support and encouragement made this milestone a joyful leap. I wish to express my grateful appreciation and admiration for my chairperson, Dr. Elizabeth Matthews whose uplifting and positive style wove much of my academic motivation. I wish to thank my son, John, for his well measured enthusiasm and patience.

ABSTRACT

Projective drawing is a language independent way of expressing personality. Previous research has indicated that projective drawing techniques are an alternative to language dependent inventories. However, there remains an important gap in the current literature regarding the specific measures used in projective techniques that correlate to personality characteristics. Therefore, the purpose of the proposed study is to determine if constructs found in projective drawing data correlate to Jungian personal typology as indicated by the Myers-Briggs Type Indicator® (MBTI®). Using 50 participants recruited from civilian, contractor, and military Integrated Product Teams, the proposed study would use a mixed-methods strategy to investigate if projective drawing data correlates with the MBTI dichotomous pairs. The mixed-method strategy begins with qualitative analysis of participants' Draw-a-Work-Group and Kinetic-Draw-a-Work-Group drawings to code a priori constructs appearing across drawings and to record the frequency of each construct in a matrix with each drawer's MBTI type. Then a phi-coefficient table is constructed and the Pearson formula is used to quantify the correlation between construct occurrence and MBTI dichotomous pairs. Findings from this research would help clarify if projective drawing constructs correlate with personality type. This would be an important contribution to the existing literature and would enhance social change initiatives through extending a language-independent personality type tool applicable for non-reading, or non-verbalizing individuals. This study will also help people forge positive social change by providing a projective approach, adapted from Jungian topology, to advance understanding and tolerance of personality diversity across language obstacles.

Relationship between Myers-Brigg Type Indicator®
Types and Projective Drawing Constructs

by

Cynthia M. Peterson

Thesis Submitted in Partial Fulfillment

of the Requirements for the Degree of

Master of Science

Psychology

Walden University

November 2008

CONTENTS

CHAPTER 1

☞

LITERATURE REVIEW

INTRODUCTION

Personality types are commonly described with visual-spatial and temporal-sequential metaphors. The proposed mixed methods study uses the Draw-a-Work-Group projective drawing directive and the Kinetic Draw-a-Work-Group projective drawing directive, to investigate if visual-spatial and temporal-sequential differences can be contextualized and correlated with the Jungian personality typology using the Myers-Brigg Type Indicator® (MTBI®). Projective techniques continue to grow in the practice of psychology as a practical alternative to forced-choice inventories; however an important gap remains in the current literature regarding the specific measures used in projective techniques that correlate to personality type within normal personality-type diversity.

The proposed methodology uses a sequential mixed-methods design with emergent theory qualitative analysis, and deductive reflection to investigate if any spatial or temporal constructs in projective drawings correlate with personality typology in a gender-heterogeneous, adult population working in diverse organizational settings. The design begins with data collection from the Draw-a-Work-Group and Kinetic-Draw-a-Work-Group projective drawing directives to create a collection of static and kinetic drawings from individuals working diverse occupations. The qualitative phase of the proposed design then uses an emergent theory methodology to discovery drawing themes that emerge from the data. The quantitative analysis phase of the methodology then uses Pearson correlation to investigate if any significant correlations exist between prominent context themes emergent from the qualitative analysis and MBTI personality preference dichotomies. Review of the literature on projective drawing in psychology shows that emergent theory methodology is consistent with methodologies used in coding projective drawing constructs (Karmiloff-Smith, 1990; Oster & Crone, 2004; Williams et al., 2006). Applying an emergent-theory research strategy, qualitative analysis of the data can reveal emergent themes from which theoretical constructs are contextualized and purposed constructs are derived (Mays & Pope, 2000).

In emergent-theory qualitative research methodology, themes emerge from the data rather than fitting data to hypothesized themes; no predetermined theoretical correlation is forced (Mays & Pope, 2000). Thus, this study begins with a literature review of emerging theories of projective drawing and its practical uses to establish background on how theoretical constructs have been contextualized in other research. The proposed study does not compile the projective constructs from previous literature to correlate with personality assessment, but rather uses emergent inquiry to arrive at particular theories pertaining to contextualizing the visual-spatial constructs emergent from the projective data.

Positive organizational cultures require tolerance, amenable environments, swiftness in decision making, and accuracy in knowledge sharing. Often during group collaboration, one reaches for a pen or whiteboard marker to explain a concept; the constructs one chooses in the communication method affect knowledge transfer among participants, each influenced by his or her personality type (Culp & Smith, 2001, Kennedy & Kennedy, 2004; Shank & Langmeyer, 1994). The proposed study adds to the literature available to organizations that use personality-type dynamics in the development of their organizational culture by purposing a strategy to investigate the theory that personality diversity projected in drawing correlates to personality dichotomies reported by the Myers-Briggs Type Indicator (MBTI).

The MBTI is one of the most popular personality inventories in use by industrial and organizational psychologists to assess the dichotomous personality factors of Jungian personality typology (Carlyn, 1977; Shank & Langmeyer, 1994) and to increase awareness and tolerance of normal personality variation organizational environments (Furnham & Crump, 2005; Logan, 1990; McCaulley, 1990; Varvel, Adams, Pridie, & Ruiz Ulloa, 2004). Organizations talk about MBTI types with visual-spatial metaphor. For example, Intuition types are described as visionary, preferring the big picture (Boyd & Brown, 2005; Craig, Duncan, & Francis, 2006), whereas Sensing types are described with nonvisual temporal terms, preferring sequences and logical flow (Craig et al.; Goby, 2006). The proposed study delves into these descriptive expectations further to investigate if individuals actually use their different visual-spatial abilities in ways that correlate to MBTI type. The proposed study investigates if such descriptive visual-spatial differences can be contextualized and correlated with the MBTI dichotomous pairs.

Personality type as given by MBTI preferences tend to correlate with occupational self-selection (Myers, McCaulley, Quenk, & Hammer,

2003). Personality type, occupational self-selection, and environmental type influence group interaction (Salter & Junco, 2007). People in the workplace often function in environments that are incongruent with the type preference; if met with opposition rather than tolerance, defenses and anxieties build (Salter & Junco). The literature has shown that individuals can hide their true personality preferences in a forced-choice assessment so as to match the expected type for a desired occupation or influence a selection outcome (Mahar, Cologon, & Duck, 1995; McFarland, 2003).

This study proposes a research strategy that expands the use of projective personality-assessment techniques in organizational settings where defenses and anxieties may skew personality-assessment results. This is important because aggressors in the workplace create an unhealthy environment in which individuals behave contrary to preferred type for an extended time and build up defenses and anxieties (Brousse et al., 2008). Defenses and anxieties are revealed less stressfully through projective techniques than through forced-choice inventory methods (Malchiodi, 2002). Because defenses and anxieties are more evident through projective techniques than forced-choice assessments (Malchiodi; Peterson & Hardin, 1997), implications of the proposed study include adding to the literature on ways organizational leaders can become aware of group dynamics and create more tolerant environments to improve their organizational culture.

ORGANIZATION OF THE CHAPTER

This chapter begins with a description of the strategy used to search literature for information about personality typology. Next, the terms used throughout the literature review are defined. Jungian theory of personality typology and the MBTI are explained prior to a brief review of the literature. The development of the MBTI is briefly discussed in general terms before the review discusses psychometrics related to dichotomous preferences scoring. Then, the use of drawing in projective testing in psychology is discussed with references to coding constructs and scoring methods.

After this foundation is built, this thesis moves into the correlating collaborative style with the dichotomous of MBTI preferences. The end of the chapter focuses on the purpose of the proposed study and the assumptions set forth by the hypotheses.

LITERATURE SEARCH STRATEGY

The literature search strategy used for this study was to use the Walden University library database library to research information from Academic Search Primer, PsycARTICLES, PsycINFO, SAGE, SocINDEX, and Google Scholar. References cited in multiple sources often aided in identifying prominently published authors in specific areas of research. The literature search started with identifying resources for theoretical background of Jungian personality typology and how MBTI builds upon Jungian theory. Past research on Jungian personality typology was then reviewed, which led to research on the development of the MBTI. Research on implications of scoring methodologies, validity, and reliability was explored, followed by current uses of the theory and MBTI in organizations. Next, research on projective drawing was reviewed with emphasis on development of coding techniques that are relevant to the proposed study. Literature was reviewed on how projective techniques for personality assessment are relevant to occupational dynamics.

Definition of Key Terms

Myers-Briggs' Introversion–Extraversion dichotomy can be defined as how an individual focuses his or her mental energies (Rosswurm, Pierson, & Woodward, 2007). *Introvert* refers to an individual who focuses his or her mental energy on constructs related to the inner world (Offir, Bezalel, & Barth, 2007). *Extravert* refers to an individual who focuses mental energy on external objects or social constructs (Francis, Craig, & Robbins, 2007).

Myers-Briggs' Judging–Perceiving dichotomy refers to the dichotomous preference of how a person interprets information from the outside world or experience (Opt & Loffredo, 2000), or whether a person prefers to use judgment or perception to organize and react to incoming stimuli (Sak, 2004). *Judging* refers to a person's preference toward using his or her judging preference rather than perceiving preference (Clack, Allen, Cooper, & Head, 2004). *Perceiving* is an individual's preference toward using the perceiving preference rather than judging preference (Ellis, 2003).

Myers-Briggs' Sensing–Intuition dichotomy refers to how a person prefers to perceive incoming information and is considered a preference of perception (Craig et al., 2006). *Sensing* type personalities prefer to rely on fact and observation that can be collected by the five senses (Goby, 2006). *Intuiting* or *Intuition* personality types prefer to think outside of the senses and relate information to abstract thinking and conceptualizations (Boyd & Brown, 2005).

Myers-Briggs' Thinking–Feeling dichotomy refers to the dichotomous preference of how a person makes decisions and is considered a judgment reference (Ross, Francis, & Craig, 2005). *Thinking* personality types prefer to reason things impersonally and often rely on logic and fact to make decisions (Wheeler, Hunton, & Bryant, 2004). *Feeling* personality types make decisions based on other people's feelings, moral standards, and social desirability (Howell, 2004).

Theory of Jungian Personality Typology

BACKGROUND ON JUNGIAN PERSONALITY TYPOLOGY

The Jungian theory of personality type differentiates individuals' preferred methods of assimilating and responding to input stimuli from their external surroundings (Fordham, 1972). The Jungian personality topology ascribes those differentiated, preferred methods to dichotomous groups and labels them as attitudes and functions (Fordham).

Jung proposed that normal personality differences are the result of behavioral patterns that are influenced by an individuals' preference in using different mental processes (Mitchell & Shuff, 1995). Through observation, Jung contextualized two basic processes in which people's minds act: perceiving and judging (Carlyn, 1977). The perceiving process was described as the act of receiving information, and the judging process as the orientation or organization of information and the development of conclusive ideas (Harrington & Loffredo, 2001). The perceiving and judging processes were each considered to be composed of two opposing polar functions: Thinking and feeling were considered to be functions of judging, and sensation and intuition were considered to be functions of perceiving (Carlyn, 1977).

Jung's typological theory considered the attitude with which people orient their energy toward their external environment to be very important and proposed that individuals exhibit either an extraverted or an introverted orientation to the outside world (Harrington & Loffredo, 2001). According to Jungian type theory, extraverted orientations lead individuals to be preoccupied with external influences, whereas introverted individuals prefer to focus on self-understanding and emotion (Opt & Loffredo, 2003).

Jung's theory described differing personality types by integrating the four possible personality functions and defined eight separate personality types (Edwards, Lanning, & Hooker, 2002). These eight personality preferences were composed of each of the preference functions and one attitude preference: (a) Extravert-Sensing-Thinking, (b) Extravert-Intuition-Feeling, (c) Extravert-Sensing-Feeling, (d) Extravert-Intuition-Thinking, (e) Introvert-Sensing-Thinking, (f) Introvert-Intuition-Feeling, (g) Introvert-Sensing-Feeling, and (h) Introvert-Intuition-Thinking (O'Roark, 1990).

JUNGIAN PERSONALITY TYPOLOGY AND THE MBTI

In the development of the MBTI, Myers and Briggs sought to create an instrument that provided an accurate way to gather psychometric data to define Jung's theory of personality type (Varvel et al., 2004). Like Jung, Myers and Briggs supposed personality to be a dynamic and flexible construct based on an individual's preferred way of responding to external influences (Carlyn, 1977).

Myers and Briggs augmented Jung's theory of personality type by adding the auxiliary function choice of perceiving or judging (Edwards et al., 2002). This was in response to Jung's undeveloped concept of type dynamics, in which he supposed that all people have the ability to use each mental process but use their preferred method most often and use the others in hierarchy, from most preferred to least preferred (Bess & Harvey, 2002). Myers and Briggs (as cited in Myers et al., 2003) proposed a dynamic interaction between each function in which an auxiliary function is always in opposition to the primary function and helps provide balance within each personality type. The inclusion of the judging or perceiving preference resulted in the addition of 8 personality types to Jung's original 8 and provided a method for the identification of 16 separate personality types (Edwards et al.).

The MBTI was designed with the intent to sort each of four personality preferences individually and to incorporate them in a hierarchy of preferred use in accordance with Jung's theory of personality type (Bess & Harvey, 2002). The instrument was configured to score a person's preferences in the dichotomous scales of Extraversion–Introversion, Sensing–Intuition, Thinking–Feeling, and Perceiving–Judging in a self-report, forced-choice question format (Opt & Loffredo, 2000). The MBTI was developed to identify which function a person prefers to use in each dichotomous category (Opt & Loffredo). The MBTI sorts individuals into 1 of 16 possible personality types, such as the Introverted-Sensing-Feeling-Judging personality type for a person exhibiting a dominant function of introverted sensing and an auxiliary function of extraverted feeling (Opt & Loffredo).

PAST RESEARCH ON JUNGIAN PERSONALITY TYPOLOGY

Myers and Briggs began development of the MBTI in 1942 and published the first version of the instrument in 1962 (Tzeng, Outcalt, Boyer, Ware, & Landis, 1984). Since then, the MBTI has been modified, revised, and updated to improve its accuracy, reliability, and validity as well as to confront problems related to social desirability and weighting with relation to gender differences (Varvel et al., 2000).

In the development of the MBTI, Myers and Briggs used their knowledge of Jungian typology and years of observed behavior to compile a series of test items they believed to identify observable behaviors related to personality type (O'Roark, 1990). From those tests, they identified which items accurately defined each scale type and used those items to construct the first forms of the MBTI (Myers et al., 2003).

Revisions have been made over time to ensure the instrument maintains the high standards set forth by its developers, including self-test forms, procedures for testing disabled or impaired respondents, and the translation of the instrument into operational formats for alternate languages and cultures (Culp & Smith, 2001; C. Lee, Kim, Seo, & Chung, 2007; Osterlind, Miao, Sheng, & Chia, 2004). The most current revision of the MBTI is a collection of the most reliable and valid items from all of the previous revisions of the MBTI integrated with several new items, all of which have been scrutinized using modern test-development procedures, such as item response theory (IRT; Harvey & Murray, 1994).

ITEM RESPONSE THEORY (IRT) AND THE MBTI

One important change in the development of the MBTI was the decision to include more accurate scoring procedures such as IRT, which suggests that item responses are related to the construct of the subject that elicits the given response (Harvey & Murray, 1994). IRT has been used primarily to score instruments that clearly define correct and incorrect responses; however, IRT also may be used to provide an accurate scoring system for instruments that reflect dichotomous results, such as right versus wrong (Reise & Waller, 1989; Zickar, Gibby, & Robie, 2004).

The developers of the MBTI used IRT to determine how likely an individual is to choose a response on a single question that reflects the individual's overall score and to define more accurately the midpoint of each bipolar preference scale (Murray, 1996). Murray concluded that using IRT in the most recent revision of the MBTI has helped define the reliability and validity of each individual item and select the most appropriate items for use in the revised instrument. Using IRT in the development and construction of the latest revision of the MBTI has helped establish a higher standard of excellence in recording sound psychometric data (Bess & Harvey, 2002).

CURRENT PERSPECTIVES ON THE JUNGIAN TYPOLOGY AND MBTI

According to Murray (1996), the reliability and validity of the MBTI have been established by a number of psychometrically sound studies. Murray also noted that there has been criticism of the reliability and validity of the method in which the MBTI is scored, due to the simplistic method used to determine individual preference choices and the theoretical bipolarity of the functions that the test is purported to delineate.

RELIABILITY

The popularity of the MBTI has prompted a large body of research concerning the instrument's internal consistency and stability (Johnson, Mauzey, Johnson, Murphy, & Zimmerman, 2001; Murray, 1996). Various studies of the MBTI have agreed that the MBTI is an acceptable instrument for measuring Jungian typology with test–retest reliability coefficients falling well within acceptable limits for each preference scale (Carlyn, 1977; Myers et al., 2003). Split-half test reliability correlations for Form M were reported as Extravert–Introvert, .90; Sensing–Intuition, .92; Thinking–Feeling, .91; and Judging–Perceiving, .92 (Myers et al., p. 160). According to Carlyn as well as Murray, the reliability of the MBTI is well established; however, both authors mentioned concerns regarding the validity of the MBTI and the underlying theory of personality type.

VALIDITY

The MBTI was developed as an instrument designed effectively to sort individuals into groups of personality type according to Jung's theory of typology; any item that clearly reflected observable evidence of Jung's theory was considered valid by the developers of the instrument (Wheeler et al., 2004). This concept is reflected in Myers and Briggs's development of possible instrument items by considering how effective each potential item was in ascertaining the type preferences of individuals with known personality types (Myers et al., 2003).

Many psychologists have considered the MBTI to be a valid test instrument due to its ability accurately to predict already observable indicators of personality type (Carlyn, 1977; Furnham & Crump, 2005). However, there has been a great deal of skepticism from some psychologists concerning the validity of the underlying construct of Jung's type theory and Myers and Briggs's interpretation of Jung's theory (Murray, 1996). Some studies have claimed that there is no true evidence pertaining to Myers and Briggs's theory of dichotomous preferences, purporting that either Myers and Briggs's theory or Jung's theory of personality type must be flawed (Costa & McCrae, 1989; Stricker & Ross, 1964). One factor analysis study conducted by Bess and Harvey (2002) concluded that there was little evidence supporting the internal validity of the factor structure of the MBTI.

Although some researchers have remained skeptical, others regard the MBTI as valid and useful as a personality inventory that accurately delineates each dichotomous preference and provides a source for valuable insight into individual personality (Furnham & Stringfield, 1993). Tischler's (1994) study of factor analysis reported the items contained within each factor group were incontrovertibly valid.

Sipps and Alexander's (1987) research comparing the MBTI to the Eysenck Personality Inventory reported significant correlation between the personality constructs identified in the two instruments. The Sixteen Personality Factor Questionnaire compares similar constructs and confirms the validity (Croom, Wallace, & Schurger,

1989). Use of IRT also has allowed more accurate measurement of the instrument's internal construct validity and has provided evidence to support the dichotomous relationship between each preference scale (Harvey & Murray, 1994).

The MBTI is one of the most popular personality inventories in use by industrial and organizational psychologists in a host of applications (McCaulley, 1990). Despite this popularity, there has been quite a bit of criticism of the instrument's validity, which some psychologists have reported to be weak or altogether nonexistent (Costa & McRae, 1989). Much of the debate concerning the validity of the MBTI is about the developers' continued use of dichotomous preference scores rather than scores that reflect the strength of preference and about lack of empirical evidence to support the four-factor construct of the instrument (Bess & Harvey, 2002). Bess and Harvey contended that even though IRT was used to score each preference scale in the most recent version of the MBTI, the midpoint of the each scale was arbitrarily defined, and the scores do not reflect the instrument's true internal validity or reliability scores. Despite their skepticism, Bess and Harvey did not claim that their results discredited the MBTI; they proposed the use of confirmatory factor analysis as a possible method of obtaining more accurate results. Wheeler et al. (2004) contended that the negative correlation scores obtained by some researchers are the result of forcing MBTI items and responses into a format that was not intended by the developers of the instrument or relevant to the theoretical construct that the test was developed to measure.

Though the MBTI has critics, the instrument is capable of providing interesting insights into individual personality (Bess & Harvey, 2002; Costa & McCrae, 1989). Moore, Dettlaff, and Dietz (2004) concluded that the MBTI helps provide useful information for individuals attempting to maximize their effectiveness as supervisors. Shank and Langmeyer's (1994) research pertaining to product and consumer personality determined that the MBTI is a very effective tool when used as an indicator of normal personality types, due to the instrument's simplicity and ease of use.

Use of Personality-Type Instruments in Organizations

Practitioners in the field of organizational psychology need a valid indicator to sort personality types if they are to implement positive social and cultural change within any organization or group interaction (Lee & Lee, 2006). Sorting personality types adds value to individuals and organizations when the method reliably relates personality traits to life and work experiences (Varvel et al., 2004). Organizational psychologists use personality assessment to provide a wide range of value to employees, managers, team members, and leaders, collaborating as diverse individuals with common work goals (McCaulley, 1990). The primary value personality assessment provides organizations is that it increases individuals' awareness of the diversity of normal personality types and allows organizations to build a culture with this awareness so as to increase tolerance of diversity and improve communication dynamics (Culp & Smith, 2001). Organizations can use their employees' awareness and tolerance of personality diversity to facilitate adaptive organizational environments (Karagiannidis & Sampson, 2002). The MBTI is a self-report personality inventory (Myers et al., 2003) commonly used by effective practitioners to sort personality types and inspire positive organizational dynamics (Culp & Smith).

The MBTI is one of the most used personality instruments and was designed to be a useful tool for researchers to understand the differences in normal personalities of individuals (Kennedy & Kennedy, 2004; Shank & Langmeyer, 1994). This makes the MBTI a useful instrument in a variety of fields, including organizational development, team building, career counseling, personal development, and the development of multicultural diversity (Logan, 1990).

The MBTI is often used to define what personality types are associated with specific psychological disorders. Opt and Loffredo (2000) used the MBTI as an instrument to help understand the relationship between personality type and communication apprehension. They noted that the relationship between individuals who prefer introversion and individuals who experience communication apprehension was highly correlated and proposed using this information to structure a therapy format that addressed the specific needs of introverted personality types in developing communication skills.

Organizational psychologists have used the MBTI to determine how individual members of team projects interact, in an effort to develop better group communication and project efficiency (Culp & Smith, 2001). Culp and Smith performed a study in 2001 to determine the effects of personality type in project groups. They discovered significant correlation between disruptions in project efficiency and divergent personality types within organizational teams. Culp and Smith used the MBTI and expert knowledge of type psychology to provide solutions that led to increased efficiency.

The MBTI also has found a niche as an effective tool for career counseling and development (Kennedy & Kennedy, 2004). Kennedy and Kennedy concluded that the MBTI is a useful and helpful tool for persons preparing to enter a career path or preparing to make a career change. Stilwell and Wallick (2000) conducted a career study that used the MBTI to classify the typical personality types of individuals attracted to specific medical career fields. Stilwell and Wallick were able to report which personality types are more likely to choose a particular specialty among medical practitioners.

The MBTI can be used positively by organizations to build a culture with awareness and tolerance of normal personality diversity (Culp & Smith, 2001) and to facilitate adaptive organizational environments (Karagiannidis & Sampson, 2002). However, the MBTI should not be used for selection criteria (Mahar et al., 1995; Myers et al., 2003). Though it is not intended to marginalize individuals by type, the MBTI literature broadcasts that certain personality types are more represented in certain occupations (Myers et al., 2003). Overrepresentation of type in certain occupations does not imply that a particular personality type is better suited for a job position, and thus personality type should not be used for selection (Myers et al.). However, individuals may be concerned with their scores being released to a hiring manager if their type is not typically associated with the position they would like to hold. An individual may even attempt to fake a personality type during testing to fit in with a certain selection setting (Bauer, Maertz, Dolen, & Campion, 1998; Mahar et al., 1995; McFarland, 2003). Even if people want to conduct a sincere personality assessment, they may have difficulty decoupling defenses or anxieties that influence their daily behavior from their preferred personality type (Malchiodi, 2002). Individuals who work in an environment contrary to their own type or in an occupation typically self-selected by another type may have difficulty answering the forced-choice format of the MBTI inventory, due to a strong divergence of preference and actual behavior (Opt & Loffredo, 2000).

How candidates perceive tests has been shown to have an impact on the scores of personality test instruments and can skew the validity of personality test measures (Barsky & Seth, 2007). Personality tests with high levels of face validity are easily faked, which can lead to distorted results in selection methods; further, personality tests with low face validity can introduce adverse impact due to organizational justice (Bauer et al., 1998). Research shows a negative correlation between conscientiousness and faking, while a positive relation is found between faking and neuroticism (McFarland & Ryan, 2000).

Typically, applicants have negative views of personality tests and are tempted to distort their answers to meet the requirements of the position for which they are applying (McFarland, 2003). Applicants are suspect to have a higher motivation to fake a personality inventory used in employee selection than incumbents (Zickar, Gibby, & Robie, 2004).

Furnham and Drakeley (2000) found that people are capable of accurately estimating their results on personality tests. Some respondents fake on questions perceived to be related to job function and respond honestly to question perceived to be unrelated.(Zickar, Gibby, & Robie, 2004). Furnham and Drakeley suggested that it would be easy for applicants to distort the results of their test results by guessing the desired result and manipulating their answers correspondingly. However, Robie (2006) found that applicants who perceived a competitive job field with a low selection did not fake on personality tests when told that the personality test would be used as a determinant in the selection process. Robie contended that personality tests legally could be used when perceived selection ratios were low and competition for the position was high, without fear of skewed test results, which might result in adverse hiring practices.

However, other studies have indicated that personality measures are generally viewed in a negative manner when used in selection processes (Harland, Rauzi, & Biasotto, 1995). Harland et al. noted that even when applicants were presented with an explanation of why completion of the personality test was necessary, the use of personality tests was still viewed negatively, and distortion of responses due to intentional faking still could be prevalent.

According to McFarland (2003), intentional faking can be discouraged by warning applicants that social-desirability detection scales will be used to check personality tests for intentional faking. McFarland found that applicants were less likely intentionally to distort their answers to personality tests if they were warned that their responses would be checked. Social-desirability scales can be used to increase the reliability and validity of personality measures used in selection processes as well as to diminish the legal consequences of using tests that may contribute to adverse impact due to faked item responses (Ellingson, Sackett, & Hough, 1999).

Projective Tests in Psychodynamic Assessment

Projective techniques have been used to decouple those defenses and anxieties that influence an individual's defensive response that leads to false answers (Malchiodi, 2002). Workplace sociodemographics significantly influence an individual's stress and anxiety (Brousse et al., 2008). Projective techniques are a way to gain information about an individual that otherwise may be hidden behind those defenses or anxieties (Peterson &

Hardin, 1997). For this reason, regardless of criticisms regarding standardization methods (Lilienfeld, Wood, & Garb, 2000), projective techniques continues to grow in the practice of psychology and psychotherapy (Coulacoglou & Kine, 1995; Dent-Brown & Wang, 2004; Edwards, 1996; Fokunishi et al., 2002; Joy & Hicks, 2004). Findings from the proposed research technique may be used as a less stressful method to uncover sociodemographic information about work groups that may be more revealing than forced-choice inventory techniques.

The main criticism of projective testing is difficulty in compiling standardization methods for congruent scoring among evaluators (Lilienfeld et al., 2000). Even the Rorschach, which is the most commonly known projective test and produced standardization to compare results, though widely used by psychologists for assessment and evaluation, draws less reliance in forensic settings in comparison to normative assessments (Sweety, 2004). Thus, the proposed research is concerned with determining if consistent identification of constructs in the projective data can be reliably agreed upon by more than one rater and if the ratings correlate with the MBTI measures of known validity.

Use and Measures of Projective drawing Testing in Psychology

The present research is concerned with organizational dynamics and a means to identify differences in preferred communication styles projected through drawing. The projective-testing measures discussed next provide insight into ways researchers have coded projective-testing evaluation systems. The coding methods discussed will provide insight into qualitative and quantitative means of identifying constructs emerging from projective drawings. However, because the present research will look for normal personality styles projected in normal collaborative-drawing methods rather than divergent characteristics, the specifics of collaborative-drawing constructs related to organizational dynamics are discussed separately. These specifics include relevance to specific occupations as well as the MBTI personality type who typically self-selects in those occupations.

Since the early ages of cave drawings, collections of symbols have been woven into drawings as a means to project thoughts that were otherwise verbally inexpressible. Graphical languages use collections of symbols and images to construct messages with spatial and temporal vibrancy. Today, at every turn graphical constructs convey messages such as danger, boundaries, and expected actions. Drivers follow universally acknowledged traffic icons. Ships are navigated through international waters following boundaries given by geographical information systems. Software developers communicate using contemporary, symbolic, modeling languages. Psychologists use drawing to gain a better projection of state of mind than can be revealed by people attempting to express themselves in words (Abraham, 1990).

Drawing gives individuals a better avenue than words for expressing their thoughts, feelings, and underlying concerns (Peterson & Hardin, 1997). Drawings are less threatening and allow a way to express suppressed emotional pain or unspoken secrets (Malchiodi, 2002). When children, adolescents, or adults feel vulnerable or fear retaliation, drawings can help externalize emotions and ideas that they otherwise could not describe (Peterson & Hardin, 1997).

Researchers and clinicians use drawings to reveal quickly important intellectual and emotional information that may not be presented through conventional psychological testing (Malchiodi, 2002). Drawing provides an enlarged framework for individuals to construct their inner world, putting symbolic meanings to their experiences; self-expression through drawing communicates tangible, illustrative ideas for coping with everyday problems (Oster & Crone, 2004). This is important to the present research because individuals in a group may be concerned with stressors related to performance assessment and selection. If asked directly to verbalize emotions regarding group relationships, an individual may suppress actual feelings and deliver carefully selected verbiage congruent with organizational culture or a defensive posture. Fear of retribution may cause a group member to withhold information about conflicts and concerns. Drawings provide an indirect palette for discussing confrontational issues that otherwise would be hidden or elusive in the verbal process (Oster & Crone).

PROJECTIVE DRAWING USED IN ART THERAPY

The findings from art therapists aid the present research by providing information on how people represent their world through graphical symbols. The field of art therapy was first developed by Naumberg (1966), who used free association and interpretation with spontaneous artwork. Rhyne (1973) developed art therapy in the humanistic movement, emphasizing art activities for self-expression and group interaction. Standards of practice and ethical considerations for art therapy have been established by the American Art Therapy Association.

Clinical techniques using drawing for assessment inquire about the clients' own interpretation of their drawings, instead of imposing the views of the clinician (Naumburg, 1987). Much like an MBTI assessment, confirming or disconfirming assessment is thus a part of the technique. It is important for the present research to consider the technique of confirming or disconfirming qualitative inferences with participants.

Art therapists have constructed developmental scoring systems for children's drawings based on sequential stages of artistic development (Leibowitz, 1999; Oster & Crone, 2004; Williams, Fall, Eaves, & Woods-Groves, 2006). Kellogg (1970) collected and examined nearly a million drawings from children looking for common images and structures.

Researchers have documented the use of drawings for assessing personality, cognitive development, and emotional characteristics (Leibowitz, 1999; Oster & Crone, 2004; Williams et al., 2006). Some notable examples are that intellectual status can be assessed by counting the number of details in a drawing and that emotions can be assessed by observation of expansiveness or constriction in the drawing (Wadeson, 1980). Highly defensive individuals create monotonous reproductions; religious themes are often portrayed in drawings by schizophrenics; and eyes, windows, and televisions often appear in the drawings of individuals experiencing paranoia (Wadeson). Exaggerated attention or extra detail to a particular body part indicates an overdeveloped concern in that area (Reynolds & Hickman, 2004).

CLOCK-DRAWING TEST

Because visuo-spatial deficits are an early sign of dementia, researchers have investigated the use of projective clock-drawing tests as a screening for the detection of delirium, dementia, and cognitive dysfunction associated with Parkinson's disease (Emre, Aarsland, & Albanese, 2004), Alzheimer's disease (Agrell & Dehuln, 1998; Ferrucci, Cecchi, & Guralnik, 1996; Lee & Lawlor, 1995; Shulman, Gold, Cohen, & Zucchero, 1993), and hospice patients (Henderson, 2007). The clock-drawing test has a high correlation with the Mini-Mental State Examination (Ferrucci et al.; H. Lee & Lawlor) in patients with various cognitive dysfunctions. In the clock-drawing test administration, the subject is asked to draw a clock from memory; the scoring is then a count of the number of digits in the correct quadrant of the drawing (Watson, Arfken, & Birge, 1993). Thus, it is a quickly administered, nonthreatening means to provide a quantitative dementia screening metric (Agrell & Dehuln).

HUMAN FIGURE DRAWINGS

Human figure drawings are useful to psychologists as a means of assessing cognitive abilities (Williams et al., 2006). A number of tests using person drawings have been developed as projective indicators of personality (Goodenough, 1926; Harris, 1963; Koppitz, 1968; Naglieri, 1988; Reynolds & Hickman, 2004).

Research has not shown a definitive correlation between specific constructs observed in the human figure drawings and definite abnormal personality traits (Hammer, 1997). Anxieties, conflicts, and attitudes are communicated through signs and symbols that are unique to the client;

therefore, a meaningful diagnosis of abnormal behavior cannot be made from indicators taken out of context (Williams et al., 2006). In contrast, the present research investigates if constructs can be determined that do correlate to the normal personality types. Participants' personality types are not in question in the proposed research; emergent constructs will be correlated empirically with reported MBTI orientations.

The following discussion of emergent constructs found the literature on human figure drawings will establish the techniques used with drawing in diagnostic processes with abnormal individuals. The qualitative and quantitative techniques used to identify emergent constructs are relevant to the present research.

DRAW-A-PERSON TEST

The Goodenough (1926) Draw-a-Man Test was the first use of human figure drawings as a projective test for assessing intelligence. The Draw-a-Man Test instructs a child to draw a picture of a man. The child's drawing is then analyzed along 51 scoring items to relate intelligence with the quality of the drawing in terms of the accuracy and number of details. Now called Draw-a-Person, the tests are primarily used as a measure of cognitive ability (Machover, 1952), indicators of emotional status (Koppitz, 1969, 1984), indicators of self-concept (Tharinger & Stark, 1990), and more recently to provide insight into personality (Williams et al., 2006).

Machover (1952) hypothesized that certain expressions in the Goodenough Draw-a-Person Test provided indicators of personality characteristics. The construction of the body parts are considered to contain suggestion of social balance and control of bodily impulses; and arms and legs are symbols of social adaptation (Machover). Intense emotions are projected in the drawing as glaring eyes, bared teeth, and presence of weapons (Hammer, 1997). Bizarre, nonhuman features as well as mysterious or religious symbols suggest poor reality testing (Hammer, 1997). Machover's Draw-a-Person Test instructs the client to draw a person; after the first drawing, the client is instructed to draw a person of the opposite gender. The majority of individuals' first drawing is of their own gender (Machover).

Harris (1963) expanded the Goodenough Draw-A-Person Test to include a drawing of a man, of a women, and of the self. The Goodenough-Harris Drawing Test used a 12-point quality scale along 73 scoring items for the drawing of the man and 71 scoring items for the drawing of the woman; scoring was indeterminate for the self picture.

Koppitz's (1968) human-figures drawing method asked a child to draw one whole figure of a person. Koppitz analytically interpreted the drawing along 30 specific indicators summed to determine a maladjustment score. Missing features indicated maladjustment, and inclusion of unusual items indicated superior mental ability or abnormal concern with the area of the body overemphasized. Naglieri's (1988) human-figures drawing method used the three drawings of the Goodenough-Harris model with an improved scoring system along 14 criteria and an expanded norm group.

Reynolds and Hickman's (2004) Draw-A-Person Intellectual Ability Test for Children, Adolescents, and Adults (DAP: IQ) is a single drawing test used to estimate IQ. DAP:IQ scoring consists of 23 criteria identified for scoring body parts, clothing, and accessories. Internal consistency and interscorer reliability of the DAP:IQ as reported by Reynolds and Hickman was confirmed by Williams et al. (2006). The DAP:IQ single drawing test is relatively easy to administer and useful as a quick screening device for individual or group administration (Williams et al.).

Standardization samples for the Draw-a-Person Test are used to contextualize individual signs of the drawings; for example, the omission of eyes is associated with unwillingness to interact with the environment (Naglieri & Pfeiffer, 1992). In addition to interpreting individual signs, the number of times a recurring construct is repeated in a drawing can be quantified and correlated with disturbances (Koppitz, 1969, 1984).

Draw-a-Person Test reliability and validity are dependent on the psychometric qualities used to interpretive the drawing and comparisons with national norms (Koppitz, 1969, 1984; Naglieri, McNeish, & Bardos, 1991). The Draw-a-Person Test interpretation scheme is based on the following three criteria: (a) Make interpretations based on constructs that differentiate between normal and deviant characteristics, (b) the frequency of reoccurring constructs should be compared with the normal sample, and (c) effects of age should be considered in the evaluation (Koppitz, 1984). Koppitz (1984) used 30 emotional indicators to differentiate children with emotional disorders from a normal sample. The sample represents the normal population on 1-year age intervals, gender, geographic region, socioeconomic status, and ethnicity (Naglieri et al.).

HOUSE-TREE-PERSON TEST

Buck's (1948) House-Tree-Person psychological projective test instructs a person to draw a house, a tree, and a person on separate sheets of paper. The instruction sequence is always the same, and no additional instruction is given (c.f., Hammer, 1958, 1969; Oster & Crone, 2004). Emotional indicators are then interpreted from the details of each drawing. For example, DiLeo (1983) associated the presences of a chimney on the house with nurturance and support. Moderate smoke drawn from the chimney indicates warmth and affection; a great deal of smoke drawn indicates household tension (DiLeo). The tree drawing, being least connected to home or self, is thought to be related to perceived environmental reinforcement, from which interpretations describe biographical situations and personal characteristics of the client (Oster & Crone). For example a very large tree indicates aggressive tendencies; a very small tree indicates feeling of inferiority (Bolander, 1977).

Fokunishi et al. (2002) used a modified version of the House-Tree-Person drawing test to examine the association between pretransplant and posttransplant psychiatric disorders in living-related transplantation in 31 living-related liver-transplant pairs and 65 living-related kidney-transplant pairs. The administrator using the House-Tree-Person technique asks the patient to place the house, tree, and person on the same page and in some type of action (Fokunishi et al.). This test was designed to place less burden on the recipients and donors, because it requires only one drawing (Fokunishi et al.). Fokunishi et al. found that a truncated tree drawing that lacked the upper part of the tree trunk was produced significantly more postoperatively and that a chi-square test showed significance between donors and recipients.

DRAW-A-FAMILY TEST

The Draw-a-Family technique, originally given by Appel in 1931 and later expanded by Wolff in 1942, asks the participant to draw a picture of his or her whole family (Oster & Crone, 2004). If names are not spontaneously noted for each family member on the drawing, the participant is asked to identify them afterward. The drawings reveal interpersonal relationships, often expressed by the relative size and placement of the family members and by substitutions or exaggeration (Harris, 1963).

KINETIC FAMILY DRAWING

Burns and Kaufman (1972) introduced the Kinetic Family Drawing test as a projective measure of perception of the dynamics of one's family by adding the directive to draw the family doing something together and by explicitly directing the individual to include themselves in the picture. The Kinetic Family Drawing test is usually administered after the Draw-a-Family test so as not to influence whether the clients leave themselves out of the Draw-a-Family drawing (Oster & Crone, 2004). The test, pertinent with children and adults, sometimes elicits the response that the family does not do anything together or shows a passive posture such as watching television (Oster & Crone). A common response shows the family at the dinner table; a lack of food present on the table indicates concerns regarding emotional nurturance (Oster & Crone). Kinetic Family Drawing can give insight into compelling interpersonal dynamics, such as when children draw themselves in proximity to parents to express status over siblings or when children represent dominance or ineffectiveness by drawing inaccurate proportions (Hammer, 1997). Facial expression in the drawings indicates whether the client perceives the family member as gentle, supportive, or harsh (Oster & Crone).

Burns and Kaufman (1972) explained that drawing constructs can indicate how affection is organized in the family, qualities of individual family members, and relationships within the family from drawings obtained from normal children as well as troubled children. Confirming that constructs can be identified from the drawings of individuals that fall within a normal characterization is import to the present research, which is concerned with normal individuals rather than deviant characteristics.

Tharinger and Stark (1990) compared qualitative and quantitative methods of scoring the Draw-a-Person Test and the Kinetic Family Drawing test. They reported that the qualitative and quantitative scoring methods significantly correlated with self-reported family functioning when the emotional indicator constructs given by Reynolds (1978) were used.

FAMILY-CENTERED CIRCLE DRAWING

Burns (1990) developed the Family-Centered Circle Drawing test that uses a series of family drawings within a large circle drawn on the page. The directive is to draw a large circle on the page; then, the client draws his or her mother in the center of the circle and symbols associated with her around the periphery of the circle. The instructions are repeated for two more pictures of the father and then the self. One more drawing is done of the parents with the client together in the circle. Observations are made as to the types of symbols, spatial relationships between parents and clients, omissions and overemphasis on bodily parts, and facial expression.

DRAW-A-GROUP TEST

Abraham (1990) presented her approach to analysis of the projective drawings collected from adults participating in her Draw-a-Group Test, in which participants are given the instruction to "draw a group, a human group in any way you like" (p. 393). She reported four basic drawing constructs: (a) forms, (b) organization, (c) content, and (d) expressivity. Then, she used the constructs to infer qualitatively correlations with the participants' psychotherapy diagnosis. Abraham's research convinced her of such a great affinity between drawing and feelings that she asserted that drawing not only facilitates psychotherapy diagnosis, but also is the genuine, natural language of human expression.

The inner group is a construct used to describe style of participation, perceptions, and attitudes towards a group (Loscertales & Guil, 1999). Abraham's (1990) research focused on the inner-group intrapsychic structure of adults who participated in group-analytic therapy. Loscertales and Guil used Abraham's Draw-a-Group model to investigate common dimensions of inner group projected in the drawing of primary school teachers and students in Seville, Spain. Loscertales and Guil referred to general patterns composing drawings as Gestalts, assigning the need to belong to a circle, tendency to maintain order to a square, and hierarchical structure to a triangle. They described frames used as boundaries, corrections as indicators of anxiety, and links as desires to form relationships.

OBJECT-REPRESENTATION PROJECTIVE TESTING

Object-relations theorists interpret personality and the interpersonal functioning by revealing individuals' ability to differentiate between their own perspective and the perspective of others (Kernberg, 2001). Researchers adapted constructs from social-cognitive theory and object-relations theory to develop coding systems to provide a quantitative way to compare groups with known interpersonal pathology with groups of normal subjects on measures of object-relational and social-cognitve processes (Stuart, Western, Lohr, & Benjamin, 1990; Westen, Lohr, Silk, Gold, & Kerber, 1990). Stuart et al. applied Blatt, Brenneis, Schimek, and Glick's coding measures of object-relational maturity to compare the Rorschach responses of subjects with a diagnosis of borderline personality disorder with normal subjects on a measure of cognitive development. Westen et al. constructed an object-relations scale designed to assess complexity of perspective coordination, affective relationship paradigms, capacity for emotional investment, and understanding of social causality. Westen (1992) used these scales to understand how patients' behavior, thoughts, and feelings are distorted by motivational and defensive processes. Schultz and Selman's (1989) empirical study applied object-relations and social-cognition theories to measure how personality factors mediate behavior. Researchers use a variety of coded measures of object relations that collectively provide evidence of reliable, content-grounded construct validity, indicating constructs that reveal data about the quality of interpersonal relationships (Blatt & Lerner, 1983).

Diguer, Pelletier, and Hébert (2004) used principal-components factor analysis of object descriptions to evaluate structural and qualitative constructs of object representations along Blatt, Wiseman, Prince-Gibson, and Gatt's (1991) characteristics scales: affectionate, malevolent–benevolent, warm–cold, degree of constructive involvement, negative positive ideal, nurturing, successful, and weak–strong. Karmiloff-Smith's (1990) studies of children's drawings of nonexistent objects identified constructs that correlate with independence and sequential constraints. Karmiloff-Smith's methods have been developed further to confirm theories of representational flexibility (Berti & Freeman, 1997; Picard & Vinter, 1996; Spensley & Taylor, 1999; Zhi, Thomas, & Robinson, 1997).

CONTEXTUALIZED THEMATIC REPRESENTATIONS OF CREATIVITY

Chen et al. (2002) contextualized scoring elements for thematic representation of cultural variations in creativity of European American and Chinese college students. Participants were asked to draw pictures titled Triangle, Rectangle, and Circle, which allowed for a wide variation of creative responses. Half of the participants was given the instruction to draw creatively; the other half was given the instruction to draw visual images in response to verbal stimuli. The instruction included, "We want you to make drawings that you personally find intuitively or subjectively appealing or 'right' to you" (Chen et al., p. 175). Chen et al. coded along four dimensions: (a) creativity, (b) uniqueness, (c) technical quality, and (d) liking. Additionally, each drawing was coded by independent coders according to seven categories of thematic contents: (a) simple, straightforward, or typical shapes; (b) decorated or three-dimensional shapes; (c) multiple shapes, embedded or arranged; (d) simple but meaningful shapes; (e) the shape in concrete context; (f) reflections of the shapes and unique perspectives; and (g) the shape in abstract context. Chen et al. used the thematic coding as a step toward contextualizing the features of the drawings in terms of the thematic representations of what the judges considered to be creative.

FRANCK DRAWING COMPLETION TEST

Franck and Rosen's (1949) projective test of masculinity and femininity used 36 incomplete, simple, line drawings as stimulus to be completed by the subject. Franck and Rosen found that men tend to close off the stimulus lines, expand the lines, and emphasize angles; women tend to leave stimulus lines open, elaborate within the stimulus, and reduce sharp angles.

Milne and Greenway (2001) used the Franck Drawing Completion Test in their study of defense style in adults. Milne and Greenway categorized drawing content into constructs that they associated with specific defenses. For example, drawings that included whole humans correlated with lower defense score on humor.

Fix (2003) used the Franck Drawing Completion Test in his study of constructs of playfulness and creativity in adults. Fix's confirmatory factor analysis showed positive correlations between two adult playfulness scales and the Franck Drawing Completion Test.

However, McCarthy, Anthony, and Domino (1970) found no correlation between the masculinity and femininity scales of an abbreviated, 12-item Franck Drawing Completion Test with the personality measures of the California Psychological Inventory and Minnesota Multiphasic Personality Inventory. Use of the abbreviated version added questions to the results that would have been reduced if the full 36-item test had been scored (McCarthy et al.).

DRAWING DIRECTIVES DERIVED

The present study is concerned with identifying constructs that correlate with preferred personality styles used in communication among normal individuals. The projective tests discussed above provide insight into ways researchers have coded evaluation systems, primarily concerned with individual and family dynamics. The proposed research is concerned with organizational dynamics and a means to identify differences in preferred communication styles through projective drawing.

The constructs discussed above give insight into how emerging constructs have been identified, which is valuable background for the present research's qualitative approach for identifying constructs emerging from the data that correlate with personality style as projected in the drawing. For example constructs associated with the Kinetic Family Drawing may emerge from the qualitative analysis, such as those given by given by Reynolds (1978): proximities, relative sizing, rotations, encapsulation, edge placement, symmetry, and stick figures. However, because the present research will look for normal personality styles projected in normal group behavior, the coding methods used for the previously discussed projective tests will not be sufficient. This discussion is given to provide awareness of possible normal constructs that may emerge from the data, not as a predetermined expectation for coding.

The tools commonly used in a person's occupation may influence choice of drawing constructs; for example, a software development professional trained to use Unified Modeling

Language would likely describe a software design using the spatial and temporal constructs of that language; a musician writing music likely would be comfortable with the temporal constructs of time signatures and meters; and a lifeguard would describe changing sea states in spatial terms of boundaries. Qualitatively to identify constructs emerging from projective drawing data, a qualitative analyst should be knowledgeable of typical drawing constructs used in the environments of study participants. An individual's typical organizational environment likely will influence his or her collaboration style (Salter & Junco, 2007; Tucker, 2008) and thus may influence the projective drawing results.

Though it is not intended to marginalize individuals by type, the MBTI literature shows that certain personality types are more represented in certain occupations (Myers et al., 2003). Often people function in environments that are in opposition to their type preference, which they may find stressful (Salter & Junco, 2007). Dimensions of environmental types influence group interaction:

extraverted environments emphasize involvement and interaction; introverted environments emphasize reflection and consideration of experiences; sensing environments focus on attention to environmental elements; intuitive environments focus on creativity and discover; thinking environments emphasize depersonalized, logical operation; and feeling environments emphasize the value of support and shared reality (Salter & Junco). Personality types emerging from qualitative analysis in the present research may be influenced by the participants' environmental experience. Thus, participant selection will include a minimal number of individuals from a minimal number of different organizational types.

THE DRAW-A-WORK-GROUP DIRECTIVE

A modification of the Draw-A-Group projective test discussed above may give the present research insight into the environment influence on the individual participant. The Draw-a-Work-Group directive will ask the participants to draw a picture or diagram of their work group. No test directive to draw whole persons will be given; the instruction will allow the participants to use stick figures, block diagrams, whole person, groups represented by geometric shapes, annotations, lists, labels, connecting lines, or any other style of drawing to represent their work group. The space will be restricted to one 8.5" x 11" blank page. After the drawing is collected, the facilitator will note the omission of labels and ask the participant to add labels if they are needed to clarify ambiguities.

The goal of the present research is to advance emergent theory from interpretation of the data on how MBTI type is correlated with drawing constructs, which then can be explored in subsequent qualitative and quantitative research. One challenge of emergent-theory, qualitative research is to allow the data to reveal the constructs and theoretical correlations (Mays & Pope, 2000). Thus, the researcher will not derive constructs from the literature on organizational or individual type preference but will prepare to recognize emerging constructs. These emergent constructs then can be triangulated with quantitative research to establish correlation with MBTI type as given in the literature. An explanation of types of constructs that may be projected in the Draw-a-Work-Group directive is given next for the purpose of explaining the goal of the research and is not intended to be a speculative prediction of constructs that will emerge from the data.

A typical way organizations represent work groups is by organizational charts, which use geometric shapes to indicate roles attached by connecting line or arrows; names of individuals filling higher roles are sometimes listed, while names of lower level employees are omitted (Molina, 2001). The present research may find group drawing constructs that represent organizational hierarchy, bureaucratic organization, encapsulation, repetitive forms, power distances, faces, decorations, borders, arrows, or indicators of kinetic flow or relationships.

MBTI types that typically self-select into roles that use organizational charts are thinking, judging, logical decision makers who extravert thinking, whether dominant or auxiliary, and introvert their preferred perceiving function, either Sensing or Intuition (Myers et al., 2003). Thus the qualitative analysis may show that thinking-judging individuals use constructs found in organizational chart-type layouts to represent their work group.

Another way a person may represent a work group is by spatial arrangement, where work group members are drawn as they typically are situated in a geographic or cultural relationship to each other. According to Shipman et al. (2001), people who share a workspace create visual representations of organizational communication. Participants for the present research will include those working on a geographically dispersed team, and thus spatial segregation of geographically separated group members may or may not be represented in the group drawing.

Roush and Atwater (1992) reported that Introverts with dominant Sensing types had the most accurate self-perceptions of MBTI types; from this Introvert-Sensing individuals could be expected accurately to detail themselves in group drawings. Intuition-Thinking, logical, and ingenious types are characterized by a dominant preference of either Intuition or Feeling, with the other as the auxiliary function, and are often described as big-picture idealists, concerned with inspiring others (Myers et al., 2003). Thus, the data may reveal that Extraverted-Intuition-Feeling types tend to draw the group without a specific figure representing themselves. Sensing-Feeling, sympathetic, and friendly types are characterized by a dominant preference of either Sensing or Feeling, with the other as the auxiliary function (Myers et al.) and tend to select into transformational leadership roles and use the most positive reinforcement with followers (Roush & Atwater, 1992). Their drawings may show attention to facial expression. Extraverted, action-oriented, cooperators whose Feeling is either dominant and extraverted or auxiliary and introverted (Myers et al.) may detail facial expressions or reconstruct a familiar group picture. The present research will look for diverse, emergent constructs from the qualitative analysis first before correlating with specific MBTI functions, orientation, or grouping of functions and orientations.

KINETIC DRAW-A-WORK-GROUP DIRECTIVE

A modification of the Kinetic-Family-Drawing projective test discussed above may give the present research insight into how different personality types describe a kinetic activity. The Kinetic-Draw-a-Work-Group directive will ask the participants to draw a picture or diagram of something that their work group or a subset of their work group does such that another similar work group could replicate the activity. No test directive on how to draw the activity will be given; the instruction will allow the participant to use annotations and any style of drawing to represent their work group. The space will be restricted to one 8.5" x 11" blank page.

Keeping in mind that the quality of qualitative analysis depends on constructs emergent from the data (Mays & Pope, 2000), no attempt will be made in advance to code constructs expected in the results. This is important because the goal of the present research is to uncover correlations in the data from which theory may emerge, rather than the data being fit to validate proposed correlations. The following discussion is given as an example vignette of the breadth of constructs and correlations that may emerge from the qualitative analysis.

Thinking-Perceiving, adaptable thinkers introvert Thinking, whether dominant or auxiliary, and extravert their preferred perceiving function, either Sensing or Intuition (Myers et al., 2003). Thinking-Perceiving types tend to have an ability to consider a broad range of facts but can have difficulty following logic shifts (Myers et al.); they are also overrepresented in the national sample in substance abuse workshops (Quenk & Quenk, 1996). Inspection of their task drawings may show more frequent constructs such as afterthoughts, changing page orientations, and erasures. The data may reveal that Introvert-Feeling, reflective harmonizers, whose Feeling is dominant and introverted or auxiliary and extraverted (Myers et al.), individualize roles. Or, perhaps, Introvert-Thinking, reflective individuals, whose Thinking is either dominant and introverted or auxiliary and extraverted (Myers et al.), tend to emphasize depersonalized roles.

Sensing-Perceiving, adaptable realists who extravert Sensing, whether dominant or auxiliary, and introvert their preferred Judging function, either Thinking or Feeling, and tend to self-select in the arts (Myers et al., 2003) may include creative details of scenery. By contrast, Sensing-Judging, realistic decision makers who introvert Sensing, whether dominant or auxiliary, and extravert their preferred Judging function, either Thinking or Feeling (Myers et al.), may supply standardized lists. These examples are given as a primer of the type of correlations that may emerge from the data; no MBTI characteristics are correlated with projective drawing constructs in the literature for normal, organizational work-group activities; the present research is proposed to fill the gaps to this end.

Summary

In summary, a review of the literature revealed that the MBTI has been established as an important instrument developed to study Jungian typology and is a valuable organizational tool that can be used reliably to relate personality traits to life and work experiences (Furnham & Crump, 2005; Logan, 1990; Varvel et al., 2004). Empirical research has shown the MBTI to be a reliable and valid instrument used to delineate between each preference of four dichotomous factor scales and identify 16 different normal personality types, according to Myers and Briggs' augmentation of Jung's personality-type theory (Carlyn, 1977; Shank & Langmeyer, 1994). The MBTI also has been confirmed as a useful and relevant test instrument that has many uses in a diverse range of practical applications in organization psychology, including team building, organizational development, career counseling, and test development (Furnham & Crump; Kennedy & Kennedy, 2004; Moore et al., 2004).

The discussion of development of projective-testing methodologies and scoring systems established that drawing constructs can be correlated with normal characteristics. Constructs may emerge from a qualitative analysis of drawings of normal individuals that may correlate to personality style.

The discussion developing the Draw-a-Work-Group and Kinetic Draw-a-Work-Group projective drawing directives elaborated on effects of environment on MBTI groupings and emphasized that individuals tend to self-select into organizational roles. The discussion further illustrated that groupings of MBTI types are described as some preferring the big picture, such as visionaries and artisans (Boyd & Brown, 2005; Craig, Bruce, & Francis, 2006), while others are described as preferring sequences, logistics, and lists (Craig et al., 2006; Goby, 2006). This further supports the expectation that individuals prefer to use their visual spatial abilities in ways that may correlate to MBTI type.

Purpose of the Proposed Study

The purpose of this proposed mixed methods study is to determine if any identifiable drawing constructs emerge from the Draw-a-Work-Group and Kinetic Draw-a-Work Group data that consistently correlate with the dichotomous MBTI functions and orientations. If specific drawing constructs correlate to personality type, subsequent qualitative and quantitative research can contextualize the data to establish processes that facilitate improvements in organizational cultures to increase tolerance of normal personality diversity and reduce workplace stress. Implications for positive social change of the proposed study are to relate the value of projective drawing techniques to the MBTI lexicon that is widely accepted in modern progressive organizational cultures.

Statement of the Problem

Past research has shown that personality type and organizational environment effects influence organizational culture (Salter & Junco, 2007; Tucker, 2008); workplace anxiety and defense mechanisms (Brousse et al., 2008) can lead to intentionally skewed personality assessment using a forced-choice inventory (Bauer et al., 1998; Mahar et al., 1995; McFarland, 2003). Research also has shown that projective drawing techniques provide a means to build awareness and decouple those defenses and anxieties in assessment (Malchiodi, 2002).

However, an important gap remains in the literature in that we still do not know if specific drawing constructs can be identified in projective drawings that correlate to personality type. Finding correlations within the normal personality-type diversity found in the workplace could lay the groundwork for further studies on projective drawing methods for use in normal organizational dynamics.

SUMMARY OF WHAT IS KNOWN

We know that projective drawing has been used by psychologists to study normal and deviant personality characteristics (Coulacoglou & Kine, 1995; Dent-Brown & Wang, 2004; Edwards, 1996; Fokunishi et al., 2002; Joy & Hicks, 2004). We also know that personality type as given by MBTI preferences correlates with occupational self-selection and may be a stressor that influences an individual to skew results of a forced-choice inventory (Bauer et al., 1998; Mahar et al., 1995; McFarland, 2003).

EXPLANATION OF THE GAP THE STUDY INTENDS TO FILL

The gap this study intends to fill is between emergent, projective drawing constructs and normal personality characteristics. This study intends to uncover constructs emergent from projective drawing that can contribute to the research of normal personality preference as applied in the organizational setting. This study intends to contribute to the literature such that understanding MBTI-type diversity in projective drawing may be used in subsequent research to contextualize constructs and make recommendations for improving tolerance of normal personality diversity in the workplace.

Qualitative Research Question

The central question in this study is the following: Do any identifiable drawing constructs emerge from the Draw-a-Work-Group and Kinetic

Draw-a-Work-Group projective drawings that consistently correlate with the dichotomous MBTI functions and orientations?

The qualitative research methods in this study are performed by collecting data, analyzing data, and interpreting data using iterations dialectic and inductive reasoning to observe patterns and develop theories for understanding emergent projective themes. The qualitative analysis method is performed in iterative cycles such that emergent themes in the exploratory investigation of the data inductively feedback to refine and add confidence in the emergent theories that will then be investigated in the quantitative phase of the sequential mixed methods design. The iterative nature of the emergent theory methodology design places the emphasis on refinement and confidence in a limited population size data set (Sandelowski, 1995).

An iterative emergent theory methodology is used in the qualitative discovery phase of the proposed research; thus the practical the number of participants is limited by iterative process (Sandelowski, 1995). The sample population for the propose research is a sample of 50 volunteers sought from diverse occupations. The proposed research population is a gender-heterogeneous, adult population, with a self-reported seventh-grade or higher English reading comprehension.

The hypotheses of the present study address the interpretive discovery of the data projected by the sample population of participants. If results merit, the emergent theory could later be generalized to a larger data set in further research. The qualitative hypotheses stated next address the potential of emergent common constructs found across the data. Discussion of the quantitative hypotheses follows in the next section.

Hypothesis 1

Null Hypothesis (H0): No identifiable drawn constructs will emerge from iterative emergent theory qualitative analysis of the Draw-a-Work-Group data for the sample population of 50 volunteers from diverse occupations.

Alternative Hypothesis (H1): Identifiable drawn constructs will emerge from iterative emergent theory qualitative analysis of the Draw-a-Work-

Group data for the sample population of 50 volunteers from diverse occupations.

Hypothesis 2

Null Hypothesis (H0): No identifiable drawn constructs will emerge from iterative emergent theory qualitative analysis of the Kinetic Draw-a-Work-Group data for the sample population of 50 volunteers from diverse occupations.

Alternative Hypothesis (H1): Identifiable drawn constructs will emerge from iterative emergent theory qualitative analysis of the Kinetic Draw-a-Work-Group data for the sample population of 50 volunteers from diverse occupations.

Quantitative Hypotheses

Upon completion of the qualitative analysis identifying dimensions of prominent contextual themes, the quantitative phase investigates if the emergent themes from the qualitative analysis correlate with the four MBTI dichotomies. The following hypotheses are made for each emergent construct identified in the data projected by the sample population of 50 participants. If results merit, further research may contribute to generalizing the findings to a larger population.

Hypothesis 3

Null Hypothesis (H0): In the population of participants, there is no correlation between the use of the drawing constructs identified by the qualitative analysis phase for individuals with the dichotomous MBTI type Extravert and the use of the drawing constructs by individuals with the dichotomous MBTI type Introvert.

Alternative Hypothesis (H1): In the population of participants, there is a correlation between the use of the drawing constructs identified by the qualitative analysis phase for individuals with the dichotomous MBTI type Extravert and the use of the drawing constructs by individuals with the dichotomous MBTI type Introvert.

Hypothesis 4

Null Hypothesis (H0): In the population of participants, there is no correlation between the use of each drawing constructs identified by the qualitative analysis phase for individuals with the dichotomous MBTI type Intuition and the use of the drawing constructs by individuals with the dichotomous MBTI type Sensing.

Alternative Hypothesis (H₁): In the population of participants, there is a correlation between the use of each drawing constructs identified by the qualitative analysis phase for individuals with the dichotomous MBTI type Intuition and the use of the drawing constructs by individuals with the dichotomous MBTI type Sensing.

Hypothesis 5

Null Hypothesis (H₀): In the population of participants, there is no correlation between the use of each drawing constructs identified by the qualitative analysis phase for individuals with the dichotomous MBTI type Feeling and the use of the drawing constructs by individuals with the dichotomous MBTI type Thinking.

Alternative Hypothesis (H₁): In the population of participants, there is a correlation between the use of each drawing constructs identified by the qualitative analysis phase for individuals with the dichotomous MBTI type Feeling and the use of the drawing constructs by individuals with the dichotomous MBTI type Thinking.

Hypothesis 6

Null Hypothesis (H₀): In the population of participants, there is no correlation between the use of each drawing constructs identified by the qualitative analysis phase for individuals with the dichotomous MBTI type Perceiving and the use of the drawing constructs by individuals with the dichotomous MBTI type Judging.

Alternative Hypothesis (H₁): In the population of participants, there is a correlation between the use of each drawing constructs identified by the qualitative analysis phase for individuals with the dichotomous MBTI type Perceiving and the use of the drawing constructs by individuals with the dichotomous MBTI type Judging.

Significance of the Study

Implications for positive social change include contributing to the methods and techniques that organizations can use to build positive organizational cultures and environments with awareness and tolerance of normal personality diversity. The proposed study builds on the widely accepted MBTI, one of the most popular personality inventories used to facilitate tolerant and diverse organizational cultures (McCaulley, 1990). The well-known lexicon of the MBTI is often incorporated into organizational culture (Kennedy & Kennedy, 2004; Shank & Langmeyer, 1994), used to maintain awareness and tolerance of normal personality diversity (Culp & Smith, 2001), and used to facilitate adaptive organizational environments (Karagiannidis & Sampson, 2002). One important factor for organizational psychology is that the MBTI was not designed to define abnormal or incongruent behaviors, but rather normal personality diversity (Wheeler et al., 2004) as found collaborating in normal, workplace, organizational dynamics. The personality types that the MBTI defines are dynamic functions of personality common to normal individual behavior (Shank & Langmeyer). Therefore, the implications for positive social change of the proposed study extend to the large population of normal individuals employed in the broad reach of organizations that have adopted use of the MBTI in their organizational culture.

The proposed study adds to the literature on projective techniques in normal personality assessment in organizational settings where known statistical correlations and desired type may skew forced-choice inventory responses (Bauer et al., 1998; Mahar et al., 1995; McFarland, 2003). Organizations that incorporate personality diversity awareness into their organizational culture can increase tolerance rather than marginalize individuals by type (Culp & Smith, 2001). However, though the MBTI is not intended to marginalize individuals by type, the MBTI type is shown to correlate with self-selection in certain roles and occupations (Myers et al., 2003), which may influence individuals to deliberately skew answers on the forced-choice personality inventory to fit a desired role or defend a current position (Bauer et al.; Mahar et al.; McFarland).

The methodology proposed in the study has implications for positive social change by potentially laying groundwork for the use of the projective techniques in normal personality assessment in organizational settings where defenses or anxieties skew assessment results (Mahar et al., 1995). Aggressors in the workplace may cause an individual to behave in an overly defense mode contrary to preferred type for an extended time, causing defenses or anxieties (Brousse et al., 2008). Defenses and anxieties are revealed less stressfully through projective techniques than through forced-choice inventory methods (Malchiodi, 2002). Defenses and anxieties are also more evident through projective techniques than through forced-choice assessments (Malchiodi; Peterson & Hardin, 1997). Implications of the proposed study include adding to the literature on ways organizational architects can become aware of group dynamics and anxieties to improve their organizational culture.

The proposed study adds to the literature on techniques that organizations can use to build positive organizational cultures and environments with awareness and tolerance of normal personality diversity. This is important because organizational collaboration requires tolerance, swiftness in decision making, and accuracy in grasping ideas. Often during collaboration, one reaches for a pen or whiteboard marker to explain a concept; the constructs one chooses in the communication method affect knowledge transfer among participants, each influenced by his or her personality type (Culp & Smith, 2001; Kennedy & Kennedy, 2004; Shank & Langmeyer, 1994). The proposed study adds to the literature available to organizations that train their employees on personality-type dynamics using the MBTI and thereby incorporate the lexicon of the MBTI into their organizational culture (Kennedy & Kennedy; Shank & Langmeyer).

The proposed methodology adds to the literature on methods of determining a coding system for projective techniques using a mixed-method approach to elucidate dichotomous components in projective testing, which subsequently may be explored with standardized methods (Lilienfeld et al., 2000; Sweety, 2004). Findings from the proposed research have implications for positive social change by laying the groundwork for understanding how personality type correlates with the coded protective measures.

Summary

The proposed study uses a mixed-method research analysis of data collected from the Draw-a-Work-Group and Kinetic-Draw-a-Work-Group projective drawing directives to investigate if visual-spatial and temporal-sequential differences can be contextualized and correlated with the Jungian personality typology using the MBTI. The MBTI provides an accurate way to gather psychometric data to define Jung's theory of personality type (Bess & Harvey, 2002; Edwards et al., 2002; Varvel et al., 2004). Projective drawing methods are another way researchers gather information about personality type. Many researchers use projective drawing methods for assessing personality, cognitive development, and emotional characteristics (Leibowitz, 1999; Oster & Crone, 2004; Williams et al., 2006). Psychometric data and contextual themes emergent from projective drawing data have been coded and related to personality style (Goodenough,

1926; Harris, 1963; Koppitz, 1968; Naglieri, 1988; Reynolds & Hickman, 2004).

The MBTI is widely used by many organizations to build a culture with awareness and tolerance of normal personality diversity (Culp & Smith) and to facilitate adaptive organizational environments (Karagiannidis & Sampson, 2002). The proposed study addresses the research question of how projective drawing constructs relevant to organizational work groups correlate to normal personality preferences indicated by the MBTI. The literature review provided background for the proposed research to relate the value of projective drawing techniques that otherwise may be hidden behind defenses or anxieties, to the MBTI lexicon that is widely accepted in modern progressive organizational cultures.

A positive finding will provide organizations a way to readily visualize differences in normal personality-type diversity that may be used to reduce anxiety in the organizational environment (Brousse et al., 2008), increase tolerance (Culp & Smith, 2001), and increase collaborative efficacy

(Kennedy & Kennedy, 2004; Shank & Langmeyer, 1994) for individuals in the workplace. Chapter 2 details the requirements for implementing the research design.

CHAPTER 2

C3

RESEARCH METHOD

INTRODUCTION

This study investigates if visual-spatial and
temporal-sequential differences can be
contextualized and correlated with the Jungian
personality typology. Findings from the proposed
research will lay the groundwork for understanding
how personality type correlates with use of visual-
spatial and temporal-sequential themes in projective
drawing. The proposed study develops mixed-
methods approach to reveal dimensions of prominent
contextual themes in the data analysis and
deductive reflection to elucidate dichotomous
components emerging from the qualitative

measures. The proposed methodology adds to the literature on methods of determining a coding system for projective drawing techniques.

The proposed study will contribute to the research on using projective drawing techniques to assess normal personality-type diversity in organizational settings where defenses, anxieties, and knowledge of statistical correlations may skew responses (Bauer et al., 1998; Mahar et al., 1995; McFarland, 2003). In this way, the proposed study adds to the literature on techniques that organizations can use to build positive organizational cultures and environments with awareness and tolerance of normal personality diversity. This is important because organizational collaboration requires tolerance, swiftness in decision making, and accuracy in grasping ideas. When collaborating in the workplace, the constructs one chooses to communicate affect knowledge transfer among participants, each influenced by his or her personality type (Myers et al., 1998). The proposed study adds to the literature available to organizations that train their employees on personality-type dynamics using the MBTI and thereby incorporate the lexicon of the MBTI training into their organizational culture (Kennedy & Kennedy, 2004; Shank & Langmeyer, 1994).

Methodology

DESIGN

The proposed study uses a sequential mixed-methods design to investigate if emergent themes from projective drawing data can be correlated with the dichotomous MBTI personality type preferences. The research methodology is conducted in three sequential phases. The first phase is data collection, the second phase is the qualitative analysis and the third phase is quantitative analysis. The first phase, data collection, administers and collects data from the Draw-a-Work-Group and Kinetic-Draw-a-Work-Group projective drawing directives. The second phase, qualitative analysis, identifies emergent themes from the data. The third phase, quantitative analysis, correlates the emergent themes from the qualitative analysis to the four

MBTI dichotomies. Each phase is described briefly next and in stepwise detail in the procedures section. The primary activity of the methodology in the data collection phase is to collect data from the Draw-a-Work-Group and Kinetic-Draw-a-Work-Group projective drawing directives. To do this, the researcher briefly explains to the participant (who has been briefed on participants' rights, matters of consent, and the voluntary nature of the participation) that he or she will be asked to create two drawings. The researcher explains that there will be no time limit; the drawings will not be scored for correctness.

For the first drawing, the Draw-a-Work-Group drawing, the researcher will instruct the participant to make a drawing or diagram of his or her work group. The researcher explains to the participant that work group consists of the group of people that the participant works with, however; the researcher must defer determining the extent of the group to the participant. For example, the participant may question if work group includes geographically distant coworkers, people on alternate time shifts, members of from other departments, customers, children, patients, bosses, or specific stakeholders. In reply, the researcher shall tell the participant that there is no right or wrong answer; the extent of the group is determined by the participant.

For the second drawing, the Kinetic-Draw-a-Work-Group drawing, the researcher will instruct the participant to make a drawing or diagram of his or her work group, or a subset of the work group, performing a task or activity. The researcher must defer determining the drawing style or diagramming methodology to the participant. For example, the participant may question if the drawing should include instructions, goals, or time sequences. The researcher explains that the drawing may include text; however, the style of drawing or diagramming methodology is determined by the participant.

The qualitative data analysis phase of the purposed methodology uses emergent theory and deductive reflection to build a relationship-matrix of emergent constructs found in the data. Templates for this phase of the methodology are given in the appendices. The procedural details of using the templates to organize the qualitative data are given in the procedures section of this document. The emphasis of the qualitative phase of the research design is on emergent theory from the specific data generated in response to the drawing directives; thus the experience is limited by research design constraints to be representative of a broader phenomenology.

The quantitative data analysis phase of the purposed methodology uses phi-coefficient and Pearson correlation to determine if the emergent themes from the qualitative phase can be contextualized and correlated with the MBTI dichotomies. A template to record the data for this phase of the methodology is given in the appendices.

PARTICIPANTS

The proposed research population is a gender-heterogeneous, adult population, with a self-reported seventh-grade or higher English reading comprehension. Participants must have a MBTI profile report or agree to take a MBTI assessment and voluntarily must agree to allow their type reporting to be used in the study.

To achieve diversity of personality types and cultures studied, the proposed study will utilize a sample of volunteers sought from diverse work groups and occupations. Determining the sample size in qualitative research is a matter of judgment (Sandelowski, 1995). The nature of this research is exploratory and open ended; thus, a small number of participants is appropriate (Sandelowski). Results of the present study will not show that the emergent constructs are universal; instead, results will present an interpretive discovery of the data projected by the participants.

Participants for the purposeful sample will be recruited from a number of diverse work groups. Purposeful selection of the work groups will consider how individuals typically self select occupations. For example, the occupation of musicians is typically self selected by individuals with an Intuition Feeling preference (Macdaid, McCaulley, & Kainz, 2005) and the occupation of software developers is typically self selected by individuals with a Sensing Thinking preference (Capretz, 2006).

The proposed sample size is 5–10 participants from 5–10 work groups. The total proposed number of participants is 50 to meet the practical expectations of the study and to allow for opportunity to include the maximum number of participants in each purposeful sampled work group.

The researcher performing the proposed study has an ethical and legal responsibility to safeguard each participant's human rights and to apply Walden University Institutional Review Board standards to protect all of the people participating in the research. Thus, the researcher of the proposed study will gain approval from the Walden University Institutional Review Board before participants are sought and the specific research is conducted.

By the federal regulations and the American Psychological Association (APA, 2002) Ethics Code, a researcher performing such study is specifically responsible for ensuring that research is conducted legally and ethically, is scientifically valid, meets selection and equitability requirements, and causes no obstruction to the rights and welfare of participants. Investigators must use reasonable judgment when assessing the risks and benefits of the research. A benefit is considered new knowledge or improved health for the research participant; a risk is considered any physical, psychological, social, legal, or economic determent (National Institutes of Health [NIH], 2002). A benefit of the purposed research to the participant is the new knowledge gained that may increase tolerance and communication in organizational dynamics; a risk is that if a participant's supervisor gained access to the data, improper conclusions or misinterpretation may occur. Thus, the data will be kept secure and protected from inappropriate disclosure. The severity and duration of a risk impact the determination of the anticipated risk (NIH, 2002). The risk of the purposed research is associated with a participant's supervisor acting unethically with regards to the collection of information that is otherwise observable on a normal, daily basis, and thus the risk is considered minimal.

Research investigators must respect participants' privacy and confidentiality (APA, 2002; NIH, 2004; Protection of Human Subjects, 2005). Researchers conducting the proposed study must establish a trusting relationship with participants to collect data in confidentiality, and that confidentiality must be upheld. Upholding confidentiality includes taking reasonable precaution to protect information during collection, transmission, and storage (APA; NIH, 2004; Protection of Human Subjects). Information that is not germane to the present research objectives will not be recorded.

Legal authorized consent must be obtained for the disclosure of information to third parties except when allowed for law for the protection of others (APA, 2002; NIH, 2004; Protection of Human Subjects, 2005). When information is obtained that a participant poses a threat to others, state statues should be consulted to determine if the researcher has a legal duty to inform authorities (NIH, 2002). As the third-party information reflected in the proposed research is about normal, functional work groups, it is very unlikely that such elevation will ensue and thus no Certificate of Confidentially under Section 301(d) of the Public Health Service Act (1946) will be obtained.

No human subject research may be conducted without legally effective informed consent of the subject or the subject's legally authorized representative (NIH, 2004). Informed consent consists minimally of a statement revealing the purpose, expected duration; description of procedures, identification of experimental procedures; a description of the risks or discomforts, a description of the benefits, disclosure of alternative procedures, a statement of confidentially of records, explanation of any compensation for research involving greater than minimal risk, researcher's contact information, and a statement the participation is voluntary and that declining from participation evokes no penalty or loss of benefit to the participant (NIH, 2004). Informed consent for the proposed study will be recorded via a short-form written document stating that the rules of Protection of Human Subjects (2005) have been presented to the participant.

The proposed research collects data that reflect information about the participants' work group and as such collects third-party information. The Office of Civil Rights (2003) referenced the Health Insurance Portability and Accountability Act in regulating access to and disclosure of individually identifiable health information. Identifying information about a human subject or a third party should be kept secure and protected from inappropriate disclosure in accordance with the act. The present research will seek voluntary consent for disclosure of the data; when appropriate consent is obtained, specific third-party information will be removed before disclosure. Thus, presentation of the data from the proposed study will recode names and labels in the presented data such that work group members are not identified specifically by name.

MEASURES

The number of times qualitative analysis identifies emergent constructs appearing in each of the drawings will be noted. Examples of constructs that may emerge from the data include borders, lists, arrows, stick figures, facial expressions, connectivity, encapsulation, extensions, hierarchical indicators, branches, nodes, repetitive themes, decorations, indicators of power distance, highlighting self, omitting self, implied emotion, creative scenery, levels of abstraction, line quality, organization, and proximity of arrangements. Constructs that recur on a number of drawings will be compiled and quantified in relation to MBTI groupings.

Construct Score: A Construct Score is the number of times a construct is indentified in the data. Following a qualitative emergent theory methodology, Construct Scores represent the frequency a construct is observed in the data. To organize the collection of possible emergent constructs, qualitative analysis will be recorded on a

Construct Scoring Card for each drawing using the format shown in Appendix A. Possible emergent construct categories, possible emergent constructs, and possible emergent subconstructs will be recorded for each drawing.

Once all drawings are scored using the Construct Scoring Card, all of the categories from each Construct Scoring Card will be listed on the Combined Construct Categories Table using the format shown in Appendix B. Similar categories are merged to form a concise list of hierarchical parent categories with combined hierarchical-child constructs and further combined subconstructs where they merge.

Construct Matrix: A Construct Matrix is a 2 dimensional matrix of construct frequency verses observation point. Using an emergent theory methodology, the Construct matrix rows contain Construct Scores and columns list the data location which is indicated by a number assigned to each drawing which is associated with the drawer's MBTI type representation. The categories, constructs, and subconstructs listed in the Combined Construct Categories Table will be resolved into constructs on the Qualitative Construct Matrix (see Appendix C). The presence or absence of each category and construct will be recorded in the matrix.

Following creation of the matrix, a Secondary Rater Matrix Score Card will be created, similar to the Qualitative Construct Matrix. The Found in Drawing Number and Subconstruct fields will be left blank, as shown in Appendix D. A rater who did not perform the original qualitative analysis will complete the Secondary Rater Matrix Score Card for each drawing, filling in the Found in Drawing Number column.

The Qualitative Construct Matrix and the Secondary Rater Matrix Score Card then will be compared. The categories and constructs where the two matrices agree will be listed on a Proposed Projective Constructs Matrix in the format of Appendix E. The personality types as given by the MBTI of the participants will be listed with the drawing number. The total number of each MBTI indicator will be compiled for each construct.

Pearson correlation: The Pearson correlation will be used to report the relationship between the occurrence of each emergent construct and MBTI type. The correlation will show a statistic representation of the relationship between occurrences within the sample population. The Pearson correlation is a ratio comparing the covariability of construct occurrence and MBTI type with the variability of construct occurrence and MBTI type occurrence. When calculating using the Pearson correlation, the measure of covariability between two products is called the sum of the product (SP). The definitional formula for the covariability is the summation of the product of each variable minus the mean of the variable. The Pearson correlation is then computed by the sum of the product divided by the square root of the product of the sum of the squares for each variable.

Phi-coefficient: When using Pearson correlation, if both variables are dichotomous the correlation between the two variables is given by the phi-coefficient. The phi-coefficient is then computing by assigning a 0 or 1 to the dichotomous variables and using the Pearson formula with the converted scores. MBTI types are given in the dichotomous pairs of Introvert paired against Extrovert, Judging paired against Perceiving, Intuiting paired against Sensing, and Thinking paired against Feeling. Construct occurrence is dichotomously either represented or not represented. Thus each dichotomous variable will be assigned a 0 or 1 and the Pearson formula will be computed with the converted scores.

Once the frequency of each proposed category and construct is totaled for each MBTI preference, the matrix will be transposed to align the four MBTI dichotomies with each identified construct in the format shown in Appendix F. A phi-coefficient and Pearson correlation then will be used to quantify the relationship between the dichotomous variables and the construct frequencies to determine if a correlation exists between the personality dichotomy and the construct dichotomy within the participant population. Appendix F shows the phi-coefficient table for the quantitative hypotheses.

Coefficient of determination: The coefficient of determination describes the strength of the relationship given in the Pearson correlation. Specifically, the coefficient of determination measures how much of the variability in one variable is determined, or predicted, by the other variable. The coefficient of determination is calculated by squaring the Pearson correlation.

PROCEDURES

The proposed study procedure administers the Draw-a-Work-Group and Kinetic-Draw-a-Work-Group projective drawing directives individually to each participant. Each participant will be informed of the anonymous and voluntary nature of the study and that he or she is free to withdraw from the study at any time; no coercion will be used to gain participants.

The proposed study will utilize a web-based interface that opens with a written version of the informed consent consisting of a statement revealing the purpose of the study; the expected duration, a brief description of procedures, a description of the risks; a brief description of the benefits, a statement of confidentially of records, explanation that no compensation is being given for participation, researcher's contact information, and a statement the participation is voluntary and that declining from participation evokes no penalty or loss of benefit to the participant, and a link to Protection of Human Subjects (2005). Informed consent for the study will be recorded via a short-form written document stating that the rules of Protection of Human Subjects (2005) have been presented to the participant.

Each participant will be asked to follow the Draw-a-Work-Group directive and Kinetic-Draw-a-Work-Group directive using one sheet of blank paper for each. The participants will be asked to seal in an envelope for hand or post delivery to the researcher the following items: the two drawings; the short-form written consent; a note indicating their contact information, occupation, place of employment, and work group name; and a copy of their MBTI report, if available. If the participant does not have a copy of the participant's MBTI report, the participant is then given an ID and password to voluntarily log in to the MBTI server portal and take the MBTI Form M assessment. Administration of the Form M assessment ethically requires facilitation by a qualified practitioner (Myers et al., 2003); as such, the researcher is responsible for ensuring proper administration of the instrument. Upon receiving the drawings and notification that the MBTI was completed, the MBTI scoring report will be retrieved from the database. Batch capabilities of the Web portal will be used to compile the MBTI data for multiple participants.

DATA ANALYSIS

The qualitative research phase of the proposed study is intended to identify emergent constructs from the data that may correlate to personality-type dichotomies in the quantitative phase. The qualitative phase will identify emergent constructs from the projective data.. Each construct then will be listed as a possible personality type indicator and scored for presence or absence in each MBTI function and orientation represented in the participant sample. The correlation of dichotomous personality-type indicator constructs for each type then will be recorded.

The sample population for the propose research is a gender-heterogeneous, adult population population of 50 volunteers sought from diverse occupations. Thus, the hypotheses of the present study address the interpretive discovery of the data projected by the sample population of participants. The 2 qualitative hypotheses are stated next followed by a discussion on the qualitative data analysis. Then the 4 quantitative hypotheses are given followed by a discussion on the quantitative data analysis.

HYPOTHESIS 1

Null Hypothesis (H0): No identifiable drawn constructs will emerge from iterative emergent theory qualitative analysis of the Draw-a-Work-Group data for the sample population of 50 volunteers from diverse occupations.

Alternative Hypothesis (H1): Identifiable drawn constructs will emerge from iterative emergent theory qualitative analysis of the Draw-a-Work-Group data for the sample population of 50 volunteers from diverse occupations.

HYPOTHESIS 2

Null Hypothesis (H0): No identifiable drawn constructs will emerge from iterative emergent theory qualitative analysis of the Kinetic Draw-a-Work-Group data for the sample population of 50 volunteers from diverse occupations.

Alternative Hypothesis (H1): Identifiable drawn constructs will emerge from iterative emergent theory qualitative analysis of the Kinetic Draw-a-

Work-Group data for the sample population of 50 volunteers from diverse occupations.

Analysis: The qualitative phase of the purposed study follows an emergent theory methodology consistent with research methodologies use to contextualize projective drawing themes in the related projective drawing research (Goodenough, 1926; Harris, 1963; Koppitz, 1968; Naglieri, 1988; Reynolds & Hickman, 2004) to determine if identifiable drawing constructs will emerge from the drawing data resultant from the Draw-a-Work-Group or Kinetic Draw-a-Work-Group directives. The qualitative analysis method is performed in iterative cycles such that emergent themes in the exploratory investigation of the data inductively feedback to refine and add confidence in the emergent theories that will then be investigated in the quantitative phase of the sequential mixed methods design. The iterative nature of the emergent theory methodology design places the emphasis on refinement and confidence in a limited population size data set (Sandelowski, 1995).

Upon completion of the qualitative analysis identifying dimensions of prominent contextual themes, the quantitative phase investigates if the emergent themes from the qualitative analysis correlate with the four MBTI dichotomies. The following hypotheses are made for each emergent construct identified in the data projected by the sample population of participants.

HYPOTHESIS 3

Null Hypothesis (H0): In the population of participants, there is no correlation between the use of the drawing constructs identified by the qualitative analysis phase for individuals with the dichotomous MBTI type Extravert and the use of the drawing constructs by individuals with the dichotomous MBTI type Introvert.

Alternative Hypothesis (H1): In the population of participants, there is a correlation between the use of the drawing constructs identified by the qualitative analysis phase for individuals with the dichotomous MBTI type Extravert and the use of the drawing constructs by individuals with the dichotomous MBTI type Introvert.

HYPOTHESIS 4

Null Hypothesis (H$_0$): In the population of participants, there is no correlation between the use of each drawing constructs identified by the qualitative analysis phase for individuals with the dichotomous MBTI type Intuition and the use of the drawing constructs by individuals with the dichotomous MBTI type Sensing.

Alternative Hypothesis (H$_1$): In the population of participants, there is a correlation between the use of each drawing constructs identified by the qualitative analysis phase for individuals with the dichotomous MBTI type Intuition and the use of the drawing constructs by individuals with the dichotomous MBTI type Sensing.

HYPOTHESIS 5

Null Hypothesis (H$_0$): In the population of participants, there is no correlation between the use of each drawing constructs identified by the qualitative analysis phase for individuals with the dichotomous MBTI type Feeling and the use of the drawing constructs by individuals with the dichotomous MBTI type Thinking.

Alternative Hypothesis (H_1): In the population of participants, there is a correlation between the use of each drawing constructs identified by the qualitative analysis phase for individuals with the dichotomous MBTI type Feeling and the use of the drawing constructs by individuals with the dichotomous MBTI type Thinking.

HYPOTHESIS 6

Null Hypothesis (H_0): In the population of participants, there is no correlation between the use of each drawing constructs identified by the qualitative analysis phase, for individuals with the dichotomous MBTI type Perceiving and the use of the drawing construct by individuals with the dichotomous MBTI type Judging.

Alternative Hypothesis (H₁): In the population of participants, there is a correlation between the use of each drawing construct identified by the qualitative analysis phase for individuals with the dichotomous MBTI type Perceiving and the use of the drawing constructs by individuals with the dichotomous MBTI type Judging.

Analysis: Because MBTI type pairs and construct occurrence (represented or not represented) are both dichotomous, the correlation between the two will be computed by assigning a 0 or 1 to each of the dichotomous variables to calculate the phi-coefficient. The assignment of 0 or 1 to the dichotomous pairs is arbitrary when using the phi-coefficient. Then the Pearson correlation will be calculated using the phi-coefficient to compute the statistic representation of the between the construct occurrence and MBTI type occurrence within the sample population. The statistical measure should not be interpreted as a proof of cause and effect. The covariability is determined by summing the products of the difference between the occurrence of each variable and mean of each variable. The Pearson correlation then calculated by the ratio of the covariability to the square of the product of the sum of the squares of each variable. Because the phi-coefficient uses an arbitrary assignment of 0 or 1 to the dichotomous pairs, the sign of the resulting correlation is meaningless. The strength of the relationship is then calculated by squaring the Pearson correlation and thus the sign drops out anyway

Assumptions and Limitations of the Study

The main assumption and limitation of the study is that effects of the participants work group environment will influence their behavior (Salter & Junco, 2007). The extent to which work group types influence drawing constructs will not be decoupled from the data. To deal with the coupled effects, multiple participants from the same work group will be sought so that recurrent themes unique to the particular work group will show prominence in the work group type. For example, if mariners tend to draw a particular ranking crew member with a specific icon, the standardized icon will become apparent more readily if multiple members of the same group are participants.

CHAPTER 3

CB

RESULTS AND DISCUSSION

INTRODUCTION

Empirical research has shown the MBTI to be a reliable and valid instrument to assess the dichotomous personality factors of Jungian personality typology (Carlyn, 1977; Shank & Langmeyer, 1994). A review of the literature on projective-testing methodologies and scoring systems revealed the projective techniques' coded, contextual themes related to personality style (Goodenough, 1926; Harris, 1963; Koppitz, 1968; Naglieri, 1988; Reynolds & Hickman, 2004). The proposed study addresses an important gap that remains in the research as to whether specific projective constructs can be identified in work group drawings that correlate to personality type within the normal personality-type diversity found in diverse workplace settings.

Review of Literature from Chapter 1

The review of the literature on Jungian personality topology showed how Jungian personality topology ascribes normal personality differences to dichotomous groups that result from behavioral patterns influenced by individuals' preference in using different mental processes (Fordham, 1972; Mitchell & Shuff, 1995). Through observation, Jung contextualized the processes of Perceiving and Judging (Carlyn, 1977). The Perceiving process was described as the act of receiving information, and the Judging process was described as how an individual organizes information to develop ideas (Harrington & Loffredo, 2003). The Judging process is composed of two the dichotomous Thinking and Feeling functions, and the Perceiving process is composed of the two dichotomous Sensing and Intuition functions (Carlyn). The literature on Jungian personality typology proposed that individuals exhibit either an Extraverted or Introverted orientation to the outside world (Harrington & Loffredo). Extraverts are preoccupied with external influences, and introverts focus on self-understanding and emotion (Opt & Loffredo, 2000).

The literature review revealed that the MBTI instrument provides an accurate way to gather psychometric data to define Jung's theory of personality type (Bess & Harvey, 2002; Edwards et al., 2002; Varvel et al., 2004). The literature describes the MBTI as a contemporary tool; revisions ensure the instrument maintains the high standards (Culp & Smith, 2001; C. Lee et al., 2007; Osterlind et al., 2004). The use of IRT to improve internal consistency of the MBTI was reviewed, along with how using IRT in the development and construction of the latest revision of the MBTI has helped establish a higher standardization (Bess & Harvey, 2002; Murray, 1996).

The literature on current perspectives on the Jungian typology and MBTI was reviewed. According to Murray (1996), the reliability and validity of the MBTI have been established; studies of the MBTI have agreed that the MBTI is an acceptable instrument for measuring Jungian typology, with test–retest reliability coefficients falling well within acceptable limits for each preference scale (Carlyn, 1977; Murray, 1996; Myers et al., 2003). The literature review found that the MBTI is considered be a valid test instrument due to its ability to accurately predict already observable indicators of personality type (Carlyn; Furnham & Crump, 2005). However, one factor analysis study (Bess & Harvey, 2002) concluded that there was little evidence supporting the internal validity of the factor structure of the MBTI. The literature review found evidence that the MBTI is valid and useful as a personality (Furnham & Stringfield, 1993; Tischler, 1994). This is important because the MBTI is one of the most popular personality inventories in use by industrial and organizational psychologists

(Kennedy & Kennedy, 2004; McCaulley, 1990; Shank & Langmeyer, 1994).

Further, the literature review found that sorting personality types adds value to individuals and organizations (Varvel et al., 2004). Organizations can build a culture with awareness of personality diversity to increase tolerance of diversity and improve communication dynamics (Culp & Smith, 2001). The literature showed a significant correlation between disruptions in project efficiency and divergent personality type within organizational teams. The MBTI is often used by organizations to build a culture with awareness and tolerance of normal personality diversity (Culp & Smith) and to facilitate adaptive organizational environments (Karagiannidis & Sampson, 2002).

The literature review uncovered that individuals concerned with their scores being released to a hiring manager when their type is not typically associated with the position they would like to hold may attempt to fake a personality test to fit in with a certain selection setting (Bauer et al., 1998; Mahar et al., 1995; McFarland, 2003). Even when people want to conduct a sincere personality assessment, they may have difficulty decoupling defenses or anxieties that influence their daily behavior from their preferred personality type (Malchiodi, 2002).

The literature review investigated projective tests used in psychodynamic assessment, finding that projective techniques have been used to decoupling those defenses and anxieties that influence an individual's defensive response (Malchiodi, 2002). This technique is important when workplace sociodemographics significantly influence individuals' stress and anxiety (Brousse et al., 2008). The literature review revealed that projective techniques are a way to gain information about an individual that otherwise may be hidden behind defenses or anxieties (Peterson & Hardin, 1997).

The review investigated the literature on how psychologists use drawing to gain a better assessment than can be revealed verbally (Abraham, 1990) and on the coding methods used for the projective tests. These coding methods provide insight into qualitative and quantitative means of identifying constructs emerging from projective drawings. The literature review revealed that drawings are less threatening than forced-choice assessments and allow a way to express suppressed emotional pain or unspoken secrets (Malchiodi, 2002; Peterson & Hardin, 1997). Researchers and clinicians use drawings to reveal quickly important intellectual and emotional information that may not be presented through conventional psychological testing (Malchiodi). Further, projective drawing provides an indirect way to expose issues that otherwise would be hidden or elusive (Oster & Crone, 2004).

The literature reviewed explored projective drawing techniques used in art therapy (Kellogg, 1970; Naumberg, 1966; Reynolds & Hickman, 2004; Rhyne, 1973; Wadeson, 1980; Williams et al., 2006); tests of visuo-spatial deficits used in assessment of early sign of dementia and patients with various cognitive dysfunctions (Agrell & Dehuln, 1998; Emre et al., 2004; Ferruci et al., 1996; Henderson, 2007; Lee & Lawlor, 1995; Shulman et al., 1986); human-figure drawing tests as projective indicators of personality (Goodenough, 1926; Harris, 1963; Koppitz, 1968; Naglieri, 1988; Reynolds & Hickman, 2004); projective testing for assessing intelligence (Machover, 1952), emotional status (Koppitz, 1969, 1984), self-concept (Tharinger & Stark, 1990) and personality (Williams et al., 2006); and estimated IQ (Reynolds & Hickman, 2004; Williams et al.). The DAP:IQ single drawing test is relatively easy to administer and useful as a quick screening devise for individual or group administration (Williams et al.), comparisons with national norms (Koppitz, 1969, 1984; Naglieri et al., 1991), emotional indicators such as household tensions (Bolander, 1977, DiLeo, 1983; Oster & Crane, 2004), psychiatric disorders (Fokunishi et al., 2002), family dynamics (Burns & Kaufman, 1972), group dynamics (Abraham, 1990; Loscertales & Guil, 1999), object-relational and social-cognitve processes (Blatt & Lerner, 1983; Schultz & Selman, 1989; Stuart et al., 1990; Westen, 1992; Westen et al., 1990), representational flexibility (Berti & Freeman, 1997; Karmiloff-Smith, 1990;

Picard & Vinter, 1996; Spensley & Taylor, 1999; Zhi et al., 1997), cultural variations in creativity (Chen et al., 2002), projective testing of masculinity and femininity (Franck & Rosen, 1949; McCarthy et al., 1970; Milne & Greenway, 2001), and collaboration style (Salter & Junco, 2007; Tucker, 2008).

Practice Implications

The practical implication of this study is that a research strategy is proposed to expand the use of current projective drawing personality assessments. The proposed study defines a methodology for using qualitative inquiry to code prominent contextual themes in the projective data. A method is proposed to triangulate the findings by correlating the dichotomous presence or absence of the identified constructs with the dichotomous functions and orientations personality type given by MBTI using phi-coefficient and Pearson correlation.

Findings from the proposed study have implications for practice by expanding the techniques that organizations can use to build positive organizational cultures. Organizational leaders can use techniques to build environments with awareness and tolerance of normal personality diversity by increasing awareness of such diversity. Findings from the proposed research have practice implications that expand the use of the projective techniques in normal personality assessment to organizational settings, where preconceptions or anxieties may skew other types of assessment results.

Future Directions

A future direction for this study includes building on the framework of the proposed methodology to contextualize emergent constructs across larger populations. Thus, scales could be standardized for further research on projective measures of personality diversity.

Another future direction for this study is to use the findings to develop a forced-choice inventory using the contextualized drawing constructs, similar to how word pairs are used in the MBTI. The results of the forced-choice inventory then would be compared with the correlated MBTI dichotomies. Further research then could address questions concerning use of drawings to develop a nonverbal, forced-choice inventory format; consistency of preferences; and how construct use in projective drawing correlates with preference for how constructs are presented in the drawings of others.

Future directions of this study also include contributing to information on what drawing constructs should be standardized for typical business collaboration. Further research could determine what constructs a software developers building a virtual environment that uses electronic collaboration tools may use in their standard selection palette.

SOCIAL CHANGE IMPLICATIONS

Social implications of the purposed are primarily that positive social change will result from increased awareness and tolerance of normal personality diversity. The methodology proposed in this study builds on the widely accepted MBTI; thus, the social implications readily extend to the large population in organizations that have adopted the use of the MBTI in their organizational culture.

The social implications of this study focus on normal personality diversity found collaborating in normal, workplace, organizational dynamics. As such, the implications for positive social change are broad for increasing awareness and tolerance of diversity to a large population in their everyday environment. Ultimately, increasing tolerance, reducing anxiety, and increasing effective communication in organizational culture improves organizational culture (Karagiannidis & Sampson, 2002), environmental dynamics (Salter & Junco, 2007) and individual well-being (Brousse et al., 2008).

Integrative Summary

The MBTI has been established as a valuable organizational tool that can be used reliably to relate personality traits improve organizational and individual awareness and tolerance of diversity (Furnham & Crump, 2005; Logan, 1990; Varvel et al., 2004). Empirical research has shown the MBTI to be a reliable and valid instrument to assess the dichotomous personality factors of Jungian personality typology (Carlyn, 1977; Shank & Langmeyer, 1994). A review of the literature on MBTI confirmed it is useful and relevant in a diverse range of practical applications used by organizations to define organizational culture and facilitate individual development (Furnham & Crump; Kennedy & Kennedy, 2004; Moore et al., 2004).

The review of the literature on projective-testing methodologies and scoring systems established that drawing constructs can be coded and correlated to personality style (Goodenough, 1926; Harris, 1963; Koppitz, 1968; Naglieri, 1988; Reynolds & Hickman, 2004). Projective drawing has been used by psychologists to study normal and deviant personality characteristics (Coulacoglou & Kine, 1995; Dent-Brown & Wang, 2004; Fokunishi et al., 2002; Joy & Hicks, 2004). However, an important gap remains in the literature in that we still do not know if specific drawing constructs can be identified in projective drawings that correlate to personality type within the normal personality-type diversity.

The review of the literature illustrated that groupings of MBTI types are commonly described with visual-spatial metaphors. Some people prefer the big picture, are visionaries, or are artisans, whereas others are described as preferring sequences, logistics, and lists. This finding further supports the expectation that individuals prefer to use their visuospatial abilities in ways that may correlate to MBTI type (Myers et al., 2003).

The literature review shows that faking behavior on personality tests is associated with opportunity and situational influences (McFarland & Ryan , 2000). There are differences in style and extremity of faking; some respondents fake on questions perceived to be related to job function more while responding honestly to question perceived to be unrelated.(Zickar, Gibby & Robie, 2004). The purposed projective drawing methods expand opportunity for researchers to compare data from respondents; differences in honesty and faking may emerge from comparison of projective data in future studies in the arena of faking assessments.

Regardless of the correlation between personality type and occupational self-selection, people in the workplace often function in environments that are in opposition to their type preference; the incongruence can be stressful, especially if met with opposition rather than tolerance (Salter & Junco, 2007). As a result, individuals may attempt to hide their true personality preferences in a forced-choice assessment (Bauer et al., 1998; Mahar et al., 1995; McFarland, 2003). Though dimensions of environmental types should not influence selection, environmental type influences group interaction (Salter & Junco). Personality-type assessment may be influenced by the participants' environmental experience (Mahar et al.). Thus, development of a projective methodology to assess personality type in the workplace environment is appropriate because projective techniques are a way to gain information about an individual that otherwise may be hidden behind defenses or anxieties (Peterson & Hardin,

1997). Because projective drawing methods project state of mind better than words (Abraham, 1990), differences in unintentionally skewed results may emerge and be of value to further studies on how environmental stressors effect results.

The Draw-a-Work-Group directive, a modification of the Draw-a-Group projective test discussed in the literature review, directs the participants to draw a picture or diagram of their work group. The instruction allows the participants to use stick figures, block diagrams, whole person, groups represented by geometric shapes, annotations, lists, labels, connecting lines, or any other style of drawing to represent their work group. The Kinetic-Draw-A-Work-Group directive, a modification of the Kinetic-Family-Drawing projective test discussed in the literature review, directs the participant to draw a picture or diagram of something that their work group or a subset of their work group does such that another a similar work group could replicate the activity.

The goal of the proposed research is to advance emergent theory from interpretation of the data to correlate projective measures with personality dichotomies. One challenge of emergent-theory, qualitative research is to allow the data to reveal the constructs and theoretical correlations (Mays & Pope, 2000). Thus, the study does not derive constructs from the literature or past research but rather allows the researcher to recognize emerging constructs. Such constructs then can be triangulated with quantitative research to establish phi-correlation with MBTI type dichotomies.

This study focuses on normal personality diversity found collaborating in normal workplace organizational dynamics. As such, the research could lay the groundwork for far-reaching efforts to increase tolerance and awareness of diversity for positive social change.

REFERENCES

Abraham, A. (1990). The projection of the inner group in drawing. *Group Analysis, 23,* 391-403.

Agrell, B., & Dehuln, O. (1998). The clock-drawing test. *Age and Ageing, 27,* 399-403.

American Psychological Association (APA). (2002). *Ethical principles of psychologists and code of conduct.* Retrieved September 22, 2007, from http://www.apa.org/ethics/code2002.html

Barsky, A., & Seth, S. K. (2007). If you feel bad, it's unfair: A quantitative synthesis of affect and organizational justice perceptions. *Journal of Applied Psychology, 92*(1), 289-295.

Bauer, T. N., Maertz, C. P., Dolen, M. R., & Campion, M. A. (1998). Longitudinal assessment of applicant reactions to employment testing and test outcome feedback. *Journal of Applied Psychology, 83*(6), 892-903.

Berti, A. E., & Freeman, N. H. (1997). Representational change in resources for pictorial innovation: A three-component analysis. *Cognitive Development, 12*(4), 501-522.

Bess, T., & Harvey, R. (2002). Bimodal score distributions and the Myers-Briggs Type Indicator: Fact or artifact. *Journal of Personality Assessment, 78*(1), 176-186.

Blatt, S. J., & Lerner, H. (1983). The psychological assessment of object representation. *Journal of Personality Assessment, 4,* 7-28.

Blatt, S. J., Wiseman, H., Prince-Gibson, E., & Gatt, C. (1991). Object representation and change in clinical functioning. *Psychotherapy, 28*(2), 273-283.

Bolander, K. (1977). *Assessing personality through tree drawings.* New York: Basic Books.

Boyd, R., & Brown, T. (2005). Pilot study of the Myers-Briggs Type Indicator personality profiling in emergency department senior medical staff. *Emergency Medicine Australiasia, 17,* 200-203.

Brousse, G., Fontana, L., Ouchchane, L., Boisson, C., Laurent, G., Bour guet, D., et al. (2008). Psychopathological features of a patient population of targets of workplace bullying. *Occupational Medicine, 58*(2), 122-129.

Buck, J. N. (1948). The H-T-P Technique: A qualitative and qualitative scoring manual. *Journal of Clinical Psychology, 4,* 317-396.

Burns, R. C. (1990). *Guide to Family-Centered Circle Drawings (F-C-C-D) with symbol probes and visual free association.* New York: Brunner/Mazel.

Burns, R. C., & Kaufman, S. H. (1972). *Actions, styles and symbols in Kinetic Family Drawings (KFD): An interpretative manual.* New York: Brunner/Mazel.

Capretz, L. F. (2006). Clues on software engineers' learning styles. *International Journal of Computing & Information Sciences, 4*(1), 46-49.

Carlyn, M. (1977). An assessment of the Myers-Briggs Type Indicator. *Journal of Personality Assessment, 41*(5), 461-473.

Chen, C., Kasof, J., Himsel, A. J., Greenberger, E., Dong, Q., & Xue, G. (2002). Creativity in drawing of geometric shapes: A cross-cultural examination with consensual assessment technique. *Journal of Cross-Cultural Psychology 33,* 171-189.

Clack, G. B., Allen, J., Cooper, D., & Head, J. O. (2004). Personality differences between doctors and their patients: Implications for the teaching of communication skills. *Medical Education, 38,* 177-186.

Costa, P., & McCrae, R. (1989). Reinterpreting the Myers-Briggs Type Indicator from the perspective of the five-factor model. *Journal of Personality, 57,* 17-40.

Coulacoglou, C., & Kine, P. (1995). The Fairy Tale Test: A novel approach in projective assessment. *British Journal of Protective Psychology, 40*(2), 10-31.

Craig, C., Duncan, B., & Francis, L. (2006). Psychological type preferences of Roman Catholic priests in the United Kingdom. *Journal of Beliefs & Values: Studies in Religion & Education, 27*(2), 157-164.

Croom, D. P., Wallace, J. M., & Schurger, J. M. (1989). Jungian types from cattellian variables. *Multivariate Experimental Clinical Research, 9,* 35-40.

Culp, G., & Smith, A. (2001). Understanding psychological type to improve project team performance. *Journal of Management Engineering, 17*(1), 24.

Dent-Brown, K., & Wang, M. (2004). Developing a rating scale for projected stories. *Psychology and Psychotherapy, 77*(3), 325-334.

Diguer, L., Pelletier, S., & Hébert, É. (2004). Personality organizations, psychiatric severity, and self and object representations. *Psychoanalytic Psychology, 21*(2), 259-275.

DiLeo, J. H. (1983). *Interpreting children's drawings.* New York: Brunner/Mazel.

Edwards, J. (1996). Examining the clinical utility of the Moreno Social Atom Projective Test. *Journal of Group Psychotherapy, Psychodrama and Sociometry, 49*(2), 51-75.

Edwards, J., Lanning, K., & Hooker, K. (2002). The MBTI and social information processing: An incremental validity study. *Journal of Personality Assessment, 78*(3), 432-450.

Ellingson, J. E., Sackett, P. R., & Hough, L. M. (1999). Social desirability corrections in personality measurement: Issues of applicant comparison and construct validity. *Journal of Applied Psychology, 84*(2), 155-166.

Ellis, A. E. (2003). Personality type and participation in networked learning environments. *Educational Media International, 40*(1/2), 101.

Emre, M., Aarsland, D., & Albanese, A. (2004). Rivastigmine for dementia associated with Parkinson's disease. *New England Journal of Medicine, 351*(24), 2509-2518.

Fordham, M. (1972). Note on psychological types. *Journal of Analytical Psychology, 17*(2), 111-115.

Fix, G. A. (2003). The psychometric properties of playfulness scales with adolescents. *Dissertation Abstracts International: Section B: The Sciences and Engineering, 64*(2-B), 999.

Fokunishi, I., Sugawara,Y., Takayama, T., Makuuchi, M., Kawarasaki, H., & Surman, O. S. (2002). Association between pretransplant psychological assessments and posttransplant psychiatric disorders in living-related transplantation. *Psychosomatics, 43*(1), 49-54.

Francis, L., Craig, C., & Robbins, M. (2007). The relationship between psychological type and the three major dimensions of personality. *Current Psychology, 25*(4), 257-271.

Franck, K., & Rosen, E. (1949). A projective test of masculinity-femininity. *Journal of Consulting Psychology, 13*(4), 247-256.

Furnham, A., & Crump, J. (2005). Personality traits, types, and disorders: An examination of the relationship between three self-report measures. *European Journal of Personality, 19*(3), 167-184.

Furnham, A. & Drakeley, R. (2000). Predicting occupational personality test scores. *Journal of Psychology, 134*(1), 103-112.

Furnham, A., & Stringfield, I. (1993). Personality and occupational behavior. Myers-Briggs Type Indicator correlates of management practices in two cultures. *Human Relations, 46,* 827-848.

Ferrucci L, Cecchi F, Guralnik J., M., (1996). *Does the clock drawing test predict cognitive decline in older persons independent of the Mini-Mental State Examination?* Journal of American Geriatric Society, *44,* 1326-1331.

Goby, V. P. (2006). Personality and online/offline choices: MBTI profiles and favored communication modes in a Singapore study. *CyberPsychology & Behavior, 9*(1), 5-13.

Goodenough, F. (1926). *Measurement of intelligence by drawings.* Chicago: World Book.

Hammer, E. F. (1958). *The clinical application of figure drawings.* Springfield, IL: Charles C. Thomas.

Hammer, E. F. (1969). Hierarchal organization of personality and the H-T-P, achromatic and chromatic. In J. N. Buck & E. F. Hammer (Eds.),

Advances in the House-Tree-Person technique: Variations and applications (pp. 1-35). Los Angeles: Los Angeles Western Psychological Services.

Hammer, E. (1997). *Advances in projective drawing interpretation.* Springfield, IL: Charles C. Thomas.

Harrington, R., & Loffredo, D. (2001). The relationship between life satisfaction, self-consciousness, and the Myers-Briggs Type Indicator. *Journal of Psychology, 135,* 439-450.

Harland, L. K., Rauzi, T., & Biasotto, M. M. (1995). Perceived fairness of personality tests and the impact of explanations for their use. *Employee Responsibilities & Rights Journal, 10*(3), 173-184.

Harris, D. B. (1963). *Children's drawings as measures of intellectual maturity.* New York: Harcourt, Brace, & World.

Harvey, R., & Murry, W. (1994). Scoring the Myers-Briggs Type Indicator: Empirical comparison of preference score versus latent-trait methods. *Journal of Personality Assessment, 62*(1), 116-129.

Henderson, M. (2007). Use of the clock-drawing test in a hospice population. *Palliative Medicine, 21*(7), 559-565.

Howell, S. H. (2004). Students' perception of Jesus personality as assessed by Jungian-Type inventories. *Journal of Psychology and Theology, 32*(1), 50-58.

Johnson, W., Mauzey, E., Johnson, A., Murphy, S., & Zimmerman, K. (2001). A higher order analysis of the factor structure of the Myers-Briggs Type Indicator. *Measurement & Evaluation in Counseling & Development, 34*(2), 96-108.

Joy, S., & Hicks, S., (2004). The need to be different: Primary trait structure and impact on projective drawings. *Creativity Research Journal, 16*(2), 331-339.

Karagiannidis, C., & Sampson, D. (2002). Accommodating learning styles in adaptation logics for personalised learning systems. In P. Barker & S. Rebelsky (Eds.), *Proceedings of World Conference on Educational Multimedia, Hypermedia and Telecommunications 2002* (pp. 1715-1726). Chesapeake, VA: Association for the Advancement of Computing in Education.

Karmiloff-Smith, A. (1990). Constraints on representational change: Evidence from children's drawing. *Cognition, 34*(1), 57-83.

Kellogg, R. (1970). *Analyzing children's art.* Palo Alto, CA: Mayfield.

Kennedy, R., & Kennedy, D. (2004). Using the Myers-Briggs Type Indicator® in career counseling. *Journal of Employment Counseling, 41*(1), 38-44.

Kernberg, O. F. (2001). Object relations, affects, and drives: Toward a new synthesis. *Psychoanalytic Inquiry, 21*(5), 604-619.

Koppitz, E. M. (1968). *Psychological evaluation of children's human figure drawings.* New York: Grune & Stratton.

Koppitz, E. M. (1969). Emotional indicators on human figure drawings of boys and girls from middle class backgrounds. *Journal of Clinical Psychology, 25*(4), 432-434.

Koppitz E. M. (1984). *Psychological evaluation of human figure drawings by middle school pupils.* Orlando, FL: Grune & Stratton.

Lee, C., Kim, K., Seo, Y., & Chung, C. (2007). The relations between personality and language use. *Journal of General Psychology, 134*(4), 405-413.

Lee, H., & Lawlor, L. H. (1995). State-dependent nature of the clock drawing task in geriatric depression. *Journal of American Geriatrics Society, 43,* 796-798.

Lee, J., & Lee, Y. (2006). Personality types and learners' interaction in a Web-based threaded discussion. *Quarterly Review of Distance Education, 7*(1), 83-94.

Leibowitz, M. (1999). *Interpreting projective drawings: A self psychological approach.* New York: Brunner/Mazel.

Lilienfeld, S. O., Wood, J. M., & Garb, H. N. (2000). The scientific status of projective techniques. *Psychological Science in the Public Interest, 1*(2), 27-66.

Logan, G. (1990). Myers-Briggs Type Indicator—Pro or con? *Journal of Counseling & Development, 68*(3), 344.

Loscertales, F., & Guil, A. (1999). Teacher's inner group and professional identity: A study based on the DAG model. *Group Analysis, 32,* 349-366.

Macdaid, G. P., McCaulley, M. H., & Kainz, R. I. (2005). *Atlas of type tables.* Gainsville, FL: Center for Applications of Psychological Type.

Machover, K. (1952). *Personality projection in the drawing of the human figure.* Springfield, IL: Charles C. Thomas.

Mahar, D., Cologon, J., & Duck, J. (1995). Response strategies when faking personality questionnaires in a vocational selection setting. *Personality and Individual Differences, 18*(5), 605-609.

Malchiodi, C. A. (Ed.). (2002). *Handbook of art therapy.* New York: Guilford Press.

Mays, N., & Pope, C. (2000). Assessing quality in qualitative research. *British Medical Journal, 320*(7226), 50-52.

McCarthy, D., Anthony, R. J., & Domino, G. (1970). A comparison of the CPI, Franck, MMPI, and

WAIS masculinity-femininity indexes. *Journal of Consulting and Clinical Psychology, 35*(3), 414-416.

McCaulley, M. H. (1990). The Myers-Briggs Type Indicator: A measure for individuals and groups. *Measurement and Evaluation in Counseling and Development, 22,* 181-195.

McFarland, L. A. (2003). Warning against faking on a personality test: Effects on applicant reactions and personality test scores. *International Journal of Selection and Assessment, 11*(4), 265-276.

McFarland, L. A, & Ryan, A. M. (2004). Variance in faking across noncognitive measures. *Journal of Applied Psychology, 85*(5), 812-821.

Milne, L. C., & Greenway, P. (2001) Drawings and defense style in adults. *The Arts in Psychotherapy, 28*(4), 245-249.

Mitchell, C. W., & Shuff, I. M. (1995). Personality characteristics of hospice volunteers as measured by Myers-Briggs Type Indicator. *Journal of Personality Assessment, 65*(3), 521-532.

Molina, J. L. (2001). The informal organizational chart in organizations: An approach from the social network analysis. *Connections, 24*(1), 78-79.

Moore, L., Dettlaff, A., & Dietz, T. (2004). Using the Myers-Briggs Type Indicator in field education supervision. *Journal of Social Work Education, 40*(2), 337-349.

Murray, W. (1996). Testing the bipolarity of the Jungian functions. *Journal of Personality Assessment, 67*(2), 285-293.

Myers, I. B., McCaulley, M. H., Quenk, N. L., & Hammer, A. L. (2003). *MBTI manual: A guide to the development and use of the Myers-Briggs Type Indicator* (3rd ed.). Mountainview, CA: CPP.

Naglieri, J. A. (1988). *Draw-a-Person: A quantitative scoring system.* San Antonio, TX: The Psychological Corporation.

Naglieri, J. A., McNeish, T. J., & Bardos, A. N. (1991). *Draw-a-Person: Screening procedure for emotional disturbance.* Austin, TX: Pro-Ed.

Naglieri, J. A., & Pfeiffer, S. I. (1992). Performance of disruptive behavior disordered and normal samples on the Draw-a-Person: Screening procedure for emotional disturbance. *Psychological Assessment, 4*(2), 156-159.

National Institutes of Health. (2002) *Human participant protections education for research teams.* Washington, DC: U.S. Department of Health and Human Services. Retrieved September 22, 2007, from http://cme.cancer.gov/c01/pdf/ hpp-rev05.pdf.

National Institutes of Health. (2004). *Research involving human subjects.* Retrieved September 23, 2007, from http://ohsr.od.nih.gov/guidelines/GrayBooklet8240

4
.pdf

Naumberg, M. (1966). *Dynamically oriented art therapy: Its principles and practice, illustrated with three case studies.* New York: Grune & Stratton.

Naumberg, M. (1987). *Dynamically oriented art therapy: Its principles and practice.* Chicago: Magnolia Street.

Office of Civil Rights. (2003). *Summary of Health Insurance Portability and Accountability Act.* Retrieved September 27, 2007, from http://www.hhs.gov/ocr/ privacysummary.pdf

Offir, B., Bezalel, R., & Barth, I. (2007). Introverts, extroverts, and achievement in a distance learning environment. *American Journal of Distance Education, 21*(1), 3-19.

Opt, S., & Loffredo, D. (2000,). Rethinking communication apprehension: A Myers-Briggs perspective. *Journal of Psychology, 134*(5), 556-570.

O'Roark, A. (1990). Comment on Cowan's interpretation of the Myers-Briggs Type Indicator and Jung's psychological functions. *Journal of Personality Assessment, 55*(3/4), 815-817.

Oster, G. D., & Crone, P. G. (2004). *Using drawing in assessment and therapy*. New York: Brunner-Routledge

Osterlind, S., Miao, D., Sheng, Y., & Chia, R. (2004). Adapting item format for cultural effects in translated tests: Cultural effects on construct validity of the Chinese versions of the MBTI. *International Journal of Testing, 4*(1), 61-73.

Peterson, L. W., & Hardin, M. E. (1997*). Children in distress: A guide for screening children's art*. New York: W. W. Norton.

Picard, D., & Vinter, A. (1996). Relationships between procedural rigidity and interrepresentational change in children's drawing behavior. *Child Development, 78*(2), 522-541.

Protection of Human Subjects, 45 C.F.R. § 46 (2005).

Public Health Service Act, 42 U.S.C. 241(d) (1946).

Quenk, N. L., & Quenk, A. T. (1996). Counseling and psychotherapy. In A. L. Hammer (Ed.), *MBTI applications: A decade of research on the Myers-Briggs Type Indicator*. Mountain View, CA: CPP.

Reise, S. P., & Waller, N. G. (1989). Computerized adaptive personality assessment: An illustration with the Absorption Scale. *Journal of Personality and Social Psychology, 57*(66), 1051-1058.

Reynolds, C. R. (1978). A quick scoring guide to the interpretation of children's Kinetic Family Drawings (KFD). *Psychology in the School, 15,* 489-492.

Reynolds, C. R., &Hickman, J. A. (2004). *Draw-A-Person Intellectual Ability Test for Children, Adolescents, and Adults examiner's manual.* Austin, TX: Pro-Ed.

Rhyne, J. (1973). *The gestalt art experience.* Monterey, CA: Brooks/Coles.

Robie, C. (2006). Effects of perceived selection ratio on personality test faking. *Social Behavior & Personality: An International Journal, 34*(10), 1233-1244.

Ross, C., Francis, L. J., & Craig, C. L. (2005). Dogmatism, religion, and psychological type. *Pastoral Psychology, 53*(5), 483-497.

Rosswurm, A., Pierson, B., & Woodward, L. (2007). The relationship between MBTI personality types and attachment styles of adults. *Psychology Journal, 4*(3), 109-127.

Roush, P. E., & Atwater, L. (1992). Using MBTI to understand self-perception accuracy. *Military Psychology, 4*(1), 17-34.

Sak, U. (2004). A synthesis of research on psychological types of gifted adolescents. *The Journal of Secondary Gifted Education, 15*(2), 70-79.

Salter, D. W., & Junco, R. (2007). Measuring small-group environments. A validity study of scores from the Salter Environmental Type Assessment and the Group Environment Scale. *Educational and Psychological Measurement, 67,* 475-486.

Sandelowski, M. (1995). Sample size in qualitative research. *Research in Nursing & Health, 18*(2), 179-183.

Schultz, L. H., & Selman, R. L. (1989). Bridging the gap between interpersonal thought and action in early adolescence: The role of psychodynamic processes. *Psychopathology, 1*(2), 133-152.

Shank, M., & Langmeyer, L. (1994). Does personality influence brand image? *Journal of Psychology, 128*(2), 157-164.

Shipman, F., Airhart, R., Hsieh, H., Maloor, P., Moore, J. M., & Shah, D. (2001). Visual and spatial communication and task organization using visual knowledge builder. In *Proceedings of the 2001 International ACM SIGGROUP Conference on Supporting Group Work* (pp. 260-269). New York: ACM.

Sipps, G. J., & Alexander, R. A. (1987). The multifactorial nature of Extraversion-Introversion in the Myers-Briggs Type Indicator and Eysenck Personality Inventory. *Educational and Psychological Measurement, 47,* 543-552.

Spensley, F., & Taylor, J. (1999). The development of cognitive flexibility: Evidence from children's drawings. *Human Development, 42*, 300-324

Stilwell, N., & Wallick, M. (2000). Myers-Briggs type and medical specialty choice: A new look at an old question. *Teaching & Learning in Medicine, 12*(1), 14.

Stricker, L. J., & Ross, J. (1964). An assessment of some structural properties of the Jungian personality typology. *The Journal of Abnormal and Social Psychology, 68*(1), 62-71.

Stuart, J. J., Western, D., Lohr, N. E., & Benjamin, J. (1990). Object relations in borderlines, depressives, and normals: An examination of human responses on the Rorschach. *Journal of Personality Assessment, 55*(1/2), 296-318.

Shulman K. J., Gold, D., Cohen, C., & Zucchero, C. (1993) Clock-drawing test drawing and dementia in the community: A longitudinal study. *International Journal of Geriatric Psychology, 8*, 487-496.

Sweety, P. A. (2004). *Current trends for Rorschach use in forensic settings* (Doctoral dissertation, Chicago School of Professional Psychology, 2005).

Tharinger, D. J., & Stark, K. D. (1990). A qualitative versus quantitative approach to evaluating the Draw-A-Person and Kinetic Family Drawing: A study of mood- and anxiety-disorder children.

Psychological Assessment: A Journal of Consulting and Clinical Psychology, 2(4), 365-375.

Tischler, L. (1994). The MBTI factor structure. *Journal of Psychological Type, 31,* 24-31.

Tucker, J. (2008). *Introduction to type and project management.* Mountain View, CA: CPP.

Tzeng, O., Outcalt, D., Boyer, S., Ware, R., & Landis, D. (1984). Item validity of the Myers-Briggs Type Indicator. *Journal of Personality Assessment, 48*(3), 255-256.

Varvel, T., Adams, S., Pridie, S., & Ruiz Ulloa, B. (2004). Team effectiveness and individual Myers-Briggs personality dimensions. *Journal of Management in Engineering, 20*(4), 141-146.

Wadeson, H. (1980). *Art psychotherapy.* New York: John Wiley & Sons.

Watson Y. I., Arfken, C. L., Birge, S. J. (1993). Clock completion: An objective screening test for dementia. *Journal of American Geriatric Society, 41,* 1235-1240.

Westen, D. (1992). Social cognition and object relations. *Psychological Bulletin, 109,* 429-455.

Westen, D., Lohr, N., Silk, K., Gould, L., & Kerber, K. (1990) Object relations and social cognition in borderlines, major depressives, and normals: A TAT analysis. *Psychological Assessment: A*

Journal of Consulting and Clinical Psychology, 2, 355-364.

Wheeler, P. R., Hunton, J. E., & Bryant, S. M. (2004). Accounting information systems research opportunities using personality type theory an the Myers-Briggs Type Indicator. *Journal of Information Systems, 18*(1), 1-19.

Williams, T. O., Fall, A., Eaves, R. C., & Woods-Groves, S. (2006). The reliability of scores for the Draw-A-Person Intellectual Ability Test for Children, Adolescents, and Adults. *Journal of Psychoeducational Assessment, 24*(2), 137-146.

Zhi, Z., Thomas, G. V., & Robinson, E. J. (1997). Constraints on representational change: Drawing a man with two heads. *British Journal of Developmental Psychology, 15,* 275-290.

Zickar, M. J., Gibby, R. E., & Robie, C. (2004) Uncovering faking samples in applicant, incumbent, and experimental data sets: An application of mixed-model item response theory. *Organizational Research Methods, 7*(2), 168-190.

APPENDIX A
CONSTRUCT SCORING CARD

Possible emergent construct category	Possible emergent constructs	Possible emergent subconstructs or details
Drawing # ___		
Spatial Relationships	Groups organized by geographic location	Map-like layout Pinpoints indicated location of work sites
Hierarchical Relationships	Organizational chart	An organization chart was indicated for each location Top level of the hierarchy was not shown
Recurring Patterns		Multiple stick figures indicated multiple people in a subgroup
Connectivity (arrows, lines, nodes)		Arrows used to connect the subgroup of stick figures

Human Figure Drawings		Whole stick figures indicated actors
		Customer indicated with heads only
		Detailed facial expressions on the customer
		Supervisors shown with glasses
		Auditors shown with hats
Line Quality		Clear
		Bold
Completeness		The entire extent of group was depicted but did not go to the resolution of each individual, (recurring stick figures depicting multiplicity)

Note. Sample card shown with example data.

APPENDIX B
COMBINED CONSTRUCT CATEGORIES TABLE

Emergent construct category	Emergent constructs	Emergent subconstructs or details
Drawing 1		
Spatial Relationships	Groups organized by geographic location	Map-like layout
		Pinpoints indicated location of work sites
	Groups organized by desk placement	
Hierarchical Relationships	Organizational chart	An organization chart was indicated for each location
		Top level of the hierarchy was not shown

Emergent construct category	Emergent constructs	Emergent subconstructs or details
	Groups and subgroups depicted in boxes	Large boxes used for supervisors
		Supervisors named
		Small, sloppily drawn boxes for coworkers
		Coworkers' names not given
Temporal Relationships	Individuals depicted by work shifts	
	Indicators of sequence	Number labels used to indicate order
		Arrows used to indicate flow
Recurring Patterns	Multiple stick figures to indicate a group	Paper-doll-looking rows
	Recurrent circles to indicate subgroups	Multiple circles as faceless heads

Emergent construct category	Emergent constructs	Emergent subconstructs or details
Connectivity (arrows, lines, nodes)	Arrows directly connecting groups	Arrow points down from supervisor to subordinate
		Arrow point to nodes indicating common goal
	Groups connected by lines meeting at nodes	Large nodes connected groups with more detail
		Small nodes connected individuals
	Group connected directly to each other with lines	
	Friends connected by arrows labeled as such	

Emergent construct category	Emergent constructs	Emergent subconstructs or details
Borders/Bound aries	Circles around subgroups	Circles around lists indicating work group assignments
		Bold line separating customers from work group
	Borders separating groups	Cubby walls drawn

Emergent construct category	Emergent constructs	Emergent subconstructs or details
Human Figure Drawings	Whole figures	Whole stick figures indicated actors
		Auditors shown with hats & clipboards
		Stick figures with emphasized body parts
		Women shown with more detail than men
		Line stick figures with large circles for bellies
		Stick figures in action

Emergent construct category	Emergent constructs	Emergent subconstructs or details
	Heads only	Customer indicated with heads only
		Detailed facial expressions on the customer
		Supervisors shown with glasses
		Geographical distance individuals shown as faceless heads
		Side views indicating seemingly introverted coworkers

Emergent construct category	Emergent constructs	Emergent subconstructs or details
	Facial expressions, details	Smile faces: eyes with happy expression
		Frown faces: angry slanted eyebrows
		Hats
		Glasses
		Ponytails
People depicted by icons or symbols	Person symbolized by organizational icon	Military symbol

Emergent construct category	Emergent constructs	Emergent subconstructs or details
	Improvisational icons	Geometric symbols
		Anamorphic symbols
		Telephone to indicate telecommuter
		Radio to indicate dispatcher
		Paint brush to indicate painter
Roles or offices depicted rather than individuals	Office labels given rather than individuals	
Lists (by name, by role)	Reliance on lists more than drawing	Entire diagram was a list with a circle around it

Emergent construct category	Emergent constructs	Emergent subconstructs or details
	List to elaborate on a symbol	Lists connected by arrows to group blocks detailing individuals by name
Line Quality	Scattered, incomplete, frustrated	
	Bold	
Completeness	Extent of group depicted: A rather small subgroup compared to other participants from the same group	Excluded geographically separated group members
		Excluded branches other then own
	Extent of group depicted: Indicate an expanded group compared to other participants from the same group	Included customers
		Included auditors
		Included family members

.

Emergent construct category	Emergent constructs	Emergent subconstructs or details
Resolution of group depicted	Used generalized groupings	
	Used redundant multiplicity to indicate estimates of numbers	
	Explicitly labeled each individual	
Presences and placement of self	Self not identified	
	Self central to drawing	
	Self branch emphasized	Place self in a midlevel on branch
	Highlighted Self	Circled self
		Self highlighted with a star

Emergent construct category	Emergent constructs	Emergent subconstructs or details
Inferences of power distance	Supervisors orientated at the top of page	
	Downward arrow pointing to inferiors	
Inferences for change	A circled note indicating potential change that would improve organization was included	
	An arrow labeled "Should be" pointing from mid-level to top of hierarchy	
	A thought bubble with a note written in it	

Emergent construct category	Emergent constructs	Emergent subconstructs or details
Inferences of disapproval	Discontented individuals indicated by frowns with arrows pointing to implied trouble makers	
	Symbols of danger	Bold X over coworker
		Skull and cross bones with arrow pointing to work station

Note. Table shown with example data.

APPENDIX C
QUALITATIVE CONSTRUCT MATRIX

Category and construct from emergent data	Found in Drawing #									
	1	2	3	4	5	6	7	8	9	...
Spatial Relationships	x		x			x			x	
Groups organized by geographic location	x		x						x	
Group organized by desk placement						x				
Hierarchical Relationships					x		x			
Organizational chart					x					
Pyramid depiction of organization							x			
[Etc.]										

Note. Matrix shown with example data.

APPENDIX D
SECONDARY RATER MATRIX SCORE CARD

Category and construct from emergent data	Found in Drawing #									
	1	2	3	4	5	6	7	8	9	...
Spatial Relationships	x			x					x	
Groups organized by geographic location	x			x					x	
Group organized by desk placement										
Hierarchical Relationships		x	x				x			
Organizational chart		x								
Pyramid depiction of organization			x				x			
[Etc.]										

Note. Matrix shown with example data.

APPENDIX E
PROJECTIVE CONSTRUCTS MATRIX

Category and construct	`Drawing # and participant's MBTI type					Total of each MBTI preference							
	1 ES TJ	2 ES FP	3 IN FP	4 IN TJ	E t c ...	E	I	N	S	T	F	J	P
Spatial Relationships	x			x	x	9	2	4	1	4	2	4	2
Organized geographic location	x			x		1	1	1	1	2	0	2	0
Hierarchical Relationship		x	x		x	8	8	5	3	3	7	6	9
Org Chart		x			x	5	7	4	3	0	6	0	8
Pyramid			x			0	1	1	0	0	1	0	1

Note. E = Extravert; I = Introvert; N = Intuition; S = Sensing; T = Thinking; F = Feeling; J = Judging; P = Perceiving. Matrix shown with hypothetical example data.

APPENDIX F
PHI-COEFFICIENT TABLE FOR QUANTITATIVE HYPOTHESES

Participant	Construct dichotomy	Personality dichotomy

Note. Construct dichotomy: Groups organized by geographic location = 1; Groups not organized by geographic location = 0. Myers-Briggs Type Inventory personality dichotomy: Extravert = 1; Introvert = 0.